LISTEN

With Your Heart

Ginny Kearney Allen

"Listen to Him"

Luke 9:35

A.M.D.G.

Ad Majorem Dei Gloriam

For the greater glory of God

THANK YOU

Joanne Gonsalves

Debbie ChandlerJohnson

Jan Henry

Terece Horton

Jennie Allen

Kevin and Michelle Allen

Kurtis Grant

Introduction

If prayer is the lifting up of our minds and hearts to God, and if it is a covenant relationship between God and man in Christ, then I would expect that, when I am willing to LISTEN, God will answer or speak with me.

I have been speaking with Him for over 20 years and have recorded what I believe I heard. This past summer I believe that God asked me to re-read all these journals and publish a book containing all the time LISTEN was mentioned. This is it. I have not been asked to market this book. Would you do this for me?

Ginny-K-Allen@hotmail.com

255 Sea Road

Kennebunk, Maine 04043

I am the mother of 5 adult children and 12 grandchilden. A cradle Catholic in the final quarter of my life, I am desirous of coming closer to God and to Mary. Time permits me to attend daily Mass, pray the rosary, confess regularly, participate frequently in morning Prayer, read spiritual books, attend Bible studies and faith sharing groups, and spend time before the Tabernacle at the local Franciscan Friary in

Kennebunk, Maine. My problems and joys are not much different from yours. I bring them to Jesus and ask for help. He answers me. He calls me to a deeper walk with Him and lets me know how I might change my life, repent and move forward. I do not always LISTEN. When I do repent He LISTENS and forgives me.

2/8/95

What is an offense?

An offense is a transgression against another.

It is not necessary to be defensive about it. If your defenses are down God will come in and protect you. If your defenses are up God will not come in and help because it will appear that He is giving you permission to be defensive. God wants us to count on Him to come to our assistance in time of need. It is necessary to pause rather than react so that you have time to LISTEN to the response God has for you. It doesn't need to make sense. You don't have to understand everything. You just need to yield your will to the will of God so that He can accomplish His purpose through you...strange as it might seem at the time. Go in peace.

6/17/95

I want you to be at peace with yourself and others. I want you to LISTEN to Me and obey My will. You ask Me often, but then you run ahead and do whatever you think is best. You are in the wrong when you do this as you have asked Me time and time again to show you My Way. My Way is that of peace, charity, fruitfulness, generosity, kindliness, love, purity and most of all gentleness. Your way generally causes hostility, harm, hurt and pain. When you rest in My Love, as in the palm of My hand, you will have the inner peace you so earnestly desire. You will feel My comfort and My Love as you have on other occasions. So often you are running ahead of

Me. I could overtake you at any time, but I don't chose to do this. I'm waiting for you to tire of doing things your way so you can really enjoy My rest and peace.

You <u>must</u> LISTEN to Me or you will become truly exhausted both physically and spiritually. I know that you feel the need to be all things to all people, but that is for Me to do, not for you. Calm down. Take a deep breath. Relax. Enjoy the beauty of the day. Go for a ride if you are asked.

....

Run along now.

4/19/96

Come sit at My feet and LISTEN. Your Jesus wants to comfort you. Place all your cares and sorrows at My feet and leave then with Me. You have been carrying them by yourself for too long. It is time that you yielded your package of problems up to Me so that you can do the work in ministry which I have been preparing for you since creation. Flow from here in MY grace and beauty and gentleness. Let others really see Me in you. You have been so weighted down lately that some people have been having problems with your behavior. ... was correct even if you didn't like her approach. You tell too many people your story and they could care less. They are also weighted down by their problems and yours seem so insignificant to them.

Run with My Love in your heart, but only in the direction I will send you and at the speed I determine. If you stay yoked to Me, you will not weary or become tired.

I show you regularly, with My heat, that I am with you. Become more conscious of these times as opportunities to be still and treasure My Love for you. ...and... are Mine. I will take care of them both. ...is doing very well and communicates with Me regularly. I have been guiding him and He generally

LISTENS.

...still needs time to believe in My Love for him. When he recognizes the gift of my generous fruitful love he will be free to love others, but not until this time.

Finish your prayer time with Me and go home and see what I may have next in store for you My love, Jesus

5/18/96

Thank you for accepting My invitation to visit Me here at the shrine of St. Anthony. He is a favorite of many who come here for healing of soul and body. I'm glad you are here even though I know you are rather tired.

....

On a more serious note, I am concerned that you are still having difficulty focusing on letting go and letting Me direct you. For a while you follow My direction and then you run along on your own. As you have seen today, I can and do have your plans change so that you can sit back and LISTEN to Me for direction.

I want you to go home from here and take a much needed nap. I will continue to speak with you as you rest and wait.

10/4/96

Dear Jesus,

I sense that You have been waiting for me to LISTEN; that You have something to tell me and I have been avoiding this.

Dear Ginny,

I love you and desire that you approach My mother and My saints in devotion for the benefit of securing a place for yourself and your family in My eternal paradise.

This can happen as you learn more about My mother and the special role she plays in My plan for the eternal salvation of all who follow in My Love, obey My commands and persevere in My truth with devotion.

Likewise,I wish that you care more deeply for all those whom I send in your direction for assistance. You often get in the way of the message I am desiring to put across through you. Delay your own thought processes and wait for My timing and for My direction as you have been trying to do for the last month or so.

My will is easy once you have agreed to put your will aside and LISTEN for directions from Me. You will find yourself in places doing for me things of which you could never even fathom in your wildest dreams.

I need you to conform your will to Mine on a moment to moment basis.

I have gradually been showing you how this is done, but I know that you are still often fearful and unsure of what it is I am really asking of you.

Go with My flow. It is grace filled and grace full. Leave the details to Me. Relax. Let go. Stop holding on so tightly to your past or worrying about your future and that of ... .

I AM in charge and I know where you are going and I will protect you from spiritual as well as corporal danger and harm.

Meditate on My passion as seen in the Sorrowful mysteries. Yes, you have been experiencing mildly some of My pain so that you can be more open and aware and sensitive to the pain of the other.

....

I am in charge. I do know what I am doing, I do love all of you and desire heaven for you all. Be patient. Be kind. Persevere. Reread all I've spoken to you. Continue learning more of My blessed mother, Mary. Model your life on her virtues and you will find the peace that passes understanding that your heart yearns for.

Complete ....with My help then give them to Me and let them go. I will heal your wounds one at a time in My time. A healthy Ginny can be a better witness for Me, but a witness through the pain which you have suffered, much of which was caused through your own faults.

Leave your pain with Me now. Go out and enjoy this beautiful day and await whatever I have in store for you, My love. Jesus

11/12/96

Dear Jesus,

I come here before Your tabernacle to ask you what it is that You want of me. What is still in Me that you want Me to confess? How can I pray better?

Dear Ginny,

I desire that you continue to love Me and pray to Me often. It pleases Me when you continue to sit before My tabernacle rather than rush outside for conversation. If I desire that you go after Mass, I will let you know that it is Me doing the asking.

Sit at My feet and LISTEN to what I want to tell you. Still your mind from thoughts concerning the world by praising Me and thanking Me. I will bless you and your family.

Yesterday I was pleased when you had Masses offered for your family members. The problem you are concerned about is in My hands. Continue to pray ... .

This is what I desire from you,

prayer. When a thought comes to your mind about a particular person, I desire that you pray at that moment for that person and I will grace him or her. The more you talk about problems the less grace is earned for them. Talk only about Me to others who are willing to LISTEN. Pray with them. Don't ask for or tell all the details–I already know them–pray for My guidance and My peace and My charity for both yourself and for others with whom you are involved.

The Lord's prayer is a perfect prayer to be said for and with others.

You have been doing My will lately in many, but not all, situations. I am, with My mother, bringing you more into a place of silence where We can speak more readily to your open heart.

Call out Our names in your pains, distresses, failures and successes. Bring Our love to others. .... Be prepared–be sincere–be pleasant–be open–be Me ... and you will see much fruit.

I know that life hasn't been easy for you lately, but you are learning more about My suffering and from this are better able to assist others in theirs.

You don't always see it, but your pride keeps getting in your way. When it does I will point it out to you Myself or through a devoted, trusted friend.

Go now in peace and continue your day knowing of My love, peace, and presence in your heart.

I love you, Ginny

12/26/96

Dear Jesus,

Thank you for sending one of your people to comfort me and pray for me. .... .

Dear Ginny,

Once again I need you to be aware of My totallove for you ... . I am in control and all will come together in

My time.

Perhaps your fear is ungrounded. It is just worry over that about which you have no control whatsoever. Relax in Me and I will provide not only the words to use, but also the posture and body language. I will not abandon you to yourself. You will not be alone. Be sure to invoke Me, My mother and the angels to surround you in a cocoon of love and peace. You will flow if only you rely on Us for your strength. Have no agenda. Be open to where the Spirit of My Love leads you. Do not be afraid to speak what you feel we are prompting you to do. Stay calm. Breathe deeply. Open your heart and I will fill it with My unconditional love …. . Show it by a beautiful smile and a calm, relaxed exterior indicative of a serene interior.

Do not be afraid; I am with you. I will call you by your own name. You will learn to die to yourself and live wholly in My will. It will not be easy on one level, but on a deeper level it will be very important for you to let your defenses down and feel your own pain and …… .

LISTEN …. . Don't stifle My Spirit by remembering old hurts and grudges and therefore inciting more pain.

Speak softly and slowly. Don't interrupt. Don't say too much at a time. Allow for pauses and reflection. Don't hurry My process.

Thank you for asking for My assistance. Forget yourself and lean on Me in prayer and thanksgiving.

Flow in grace and peace.

Know that I love you.

1/17/97

Dear Jesus,

You have invited us to ask, seek, and knock and you will answer. I am concerned about Your will for me in regard to .... Please help me. I really do want to do what You will.

Dearest Ginny,

Because you have come to Me with your deepest desires concerning your family matters, I do want you to know of My concern and My devotion and My Love for not only you, but for all of your family. Often you are performing out of My will in regards to them because your passions and your desires get the better of you. You have confessed these and are sincerely desirous of change, I know. Please be patient with yourself. You need to stop as you have been trying to do and offer up a quick prayer before you respond. Your guardian angel, My mother and I can help you with this if you remember to ask or to LISTEN when we remind you.

Go to the party. Enjoy yourself. Don't speak of your problems with anyone and you will find the peace and serenity which you desire. Keep your conversations light and lively and off anything which might cause controversy. Allow … .

Flow as I've asked before. Be open to My inspirations. If I ask you for a change, be available and do it. You may not see any results at the time, but know that when you do My will your reward will be in Heaven.

Perhaps it would be best if you left your emotions on hold for the whole evening. Don't allow them to get the better of you. Relax! Be yourself. Have a good time! Don't worry. Be happy and you will exhibit to others the changes which have been taking place within you. You are a treasure and you need to be aware of this.

At the same time you are nothing without Me.

Thank you for coming here to the monastery to converse with Me. Go forth in peace to bring My Love, My life, and My peace to others whom you touch. Die to yourself and live wholly in Me.

1/31/97

Dear Jesus,

Is there something You want to say to me or something You would want me to do? I desire to be available to do Your will.

Dear Ginny,

Once again I thank you for coming before Me in the Blessed Sacrament to offer to do My will.

You are often in your own way as you bungle along, but, for a while now, you have been improving your position and trying more and more to LISTEN to me.

Come with Me wherever I lead and sense My presence with you. Get more and more into a mode of obedience and submission to Me. Free yourself from any schedules that are not flexible enough for Me to intervene and to change your direction at a moment's notice. I desire more praise and thanksgiving from you and less and less of you desiring and needing this praise and thanks from others for you.

Recognize Me in the moments of frenzy as well as solitude, and accept My peace for you in the middle of your circumstances.

Go forth in whatever direction I lead you and be open to My direction for you.

I bless you and hold you in My arms as does My mother, Mary.

3/5/97

I desire that you be free of the self you keep clinging to. Just now you said you were at the end of your rope again, and again I told you to let go. How often must I speak to you about trusting in Me? One day you LISTEN and the next you are off on your own again. Please stop talking about or even thinking about what you consider to be problems. Lean into Me as you leave your heart in Mine and your understanding will not matter. I do speak with you. Just be silent, LISTEN and obey.

I love you, Ginny

3/6/97

Lord, I want to love You and others, but I keep falling short of the mark. Please help me.

Dear Ginny,

Without My strength or grace, you are unable to love at all. When you place your trust in Me wholeheartedly, you will sense within yourself the push of My Holy Spirit when I choose you for a loving kindness. Hold back on all chores and ideas that are strictly from yourself. Stop and check them out with Me for confirmation. At the present time you are waiting for an answer of whether you should attend the retreat this weekend. Yes, I am not ready to give you a definitive answer. You will know when I make the decision. Don't be so worried. There will be no mistake if you truly LISTEN to Me.

I will give the circumstances in

which to practice My Love and the strenght to carry it out. Don't go looking, the situations will find you.

3/7/97

I seemed very tired and didn't sense any real connection with God. Asked for Carol Mc Laughlin's intercession for gentleness. Is there any thing else for me now, Jesus?

Dear Ginny,

Just know that, as you continue to be still and LISTEN, I will speak when I want you to LISTEN to Me. Just relax.

3/14/97

Dear Jesus,

How do I come to having inner peace?

Dearest Ginny,

You keep asking the same questions over and over. When will you appreciate what I have already said? This peace comes when you hear, LISTEN, read and then apply My Word to your situation.

Each day you will see the situation as different and difficult. Although the circumstances may change, I have already given you all you need to cooperate with Me in overcoming them. If you need more, I will give this to you also. Often I have told you to rest in Me. I have given you the picture of eagles' wings. These have been with you since you were a little child.

3/20/97

Dear Jesus,

I'm trying to Listen, perhaps you are not speaking to me today.

Dear Ginny,

I always speak to you, but you are not always receptive to what I am saying. Today I have told you that I am with you and will not leave you. You find this difficult to accept because, in your human way, all those who have loved you have left you in one way or another.

I will never leave you or forsake you. You must continue to ask, seek, and knock and expect an answer from Me. It may be in a "no", or a confirmation, or a sensation, or an awareness. Even in the dark I am there. Never forget this. You can call on Me at anytime, anywhere, and I will never be too busy. Relax. Go in My Peace and love others with My Love as I love you. Jesus

I realized the next day that I abandoned me.

Come to Me, bend with Me, eat with Me, consume Me, be My beloved. Fill yourself with my joy that you may bring it to others. Feel their pain as I've said before, bind their wounds, lighten their loads—be Me to them—whomever I put in your path—Don't push or shove just be open and LISTEN and then respond as I direct you. You are learning, but have a long way still to go. I will be with you to give you My strength (grace) and My guidance. Abide in Me and My Love and you will be filled with

My peace and security.

I love you, Ginny, Jesus

3/30/97

L

Dearest Ginny,

Rest in Me, I repeat. When you are really able to do this, I will no longer have to wait for you to be available to LISTEN, you will always be tuned into Me and My desires of you.

Keep desiring this rest and soon you will recognize it as a full time experience. It will be that peace that passes understanding. It will be calmness in the midst of turmoil. It will be relaxation in a moment that once caused you anger, bitterness and resentment. It will be so wonderful you will want to share it with everyone you meet. It will be a piece of heaven on earth.

I bless you and love you

5/5/97

Dear Jesus,

I am being annoyed by thoughts that I don't know how to pray, my prayers have no value and that when I feel the urge to comfort someone, that it is only myself. What should I do?

Dear Ginny,

Keep on praying right through the

annoyances. I am with you and am aware of all these difficulties you are having. It is one of the ways in which I am refining you so that you will persevere.

You are still talking too much and too often, but have learned something of silence in the last few weeks.

When the Bible study ends at your house this week you will feel at a loss but also a freedom. Thank you for listening.

I love you, Ginny, Jesus

5/6/97

Dear Jesus,

If the heavy-laden come to me, what

am I to do?

Dearest Ginny,

They have already been coming to you , but you don't always recognize them.

Often you talk at them when what they need is what you have been needing from Me and others– a LISTENING ear, a warm comforting embrace and an affirmation given with and in prayer.

Don't hesitate to open your Bible for a word of strength or encouragement. Have your calligraphy pen and paper handy and send them home with My Words, not yours. Be yourself, but be still more quiet and gentle. Love as I have loved you and others and you will find rest.

5/8/97

Dear Lord,

I receive often conflicting messages from others. Some say I have so much free time I ought to get a job or volunteer etc., but I think You want me available. Please help me.

Dear Ginny,

As ... said, I am the one to whom you should LISTEN. I have allowed you to live deprived of your rest these past few days so that you would thank Me for it when you are refreshed. When I have sent others to you, you have been more relaxed of late. If you were involved in more scheduled activity you would not have been available. Continue as you are in process of slowing down and you will soon see the benefits in a tangible way.

LISTEN and obey Me and you will be fruitful

and My works will multiply.

God blesses you. Amen

5/9/97

Dear Lord Jesus,

Am I presuming to ask Your guidance as I prepare to look at cars and perhaps buy one?

Dear Ginny,

As you know I am concerned about all the facets of your life. In this instance it is up to you to decide as there is no moral issue involved.

Use all the ideas I have given you in your transaction. Be more still, LISTEN, pray, be Me to those you meet. Don't compromise any of your principles, but behave in a way that all involved will be aware of their own dignity. If I have any instructions for you, just be aware of My voice in the midst of chaos and turmoil without.

I go with you.

5/10/97

Dear Jesus,

Wow–Thank you this calming message. (One I read before writing.)

Dear Ginny,

This is the message I have been attempting to relay to you for a long time, but you have been too busy and too agitated to LISTEN.

As you have become more still and recognized My voice among all the others, you have become more calm and peaceful and peace filled. It shows in your face and in your demeanor.

Trust in Me more and more and you

will have the serenity which you so desire. The trials and temptations will even increase, but you will give glory to Me in their midst as you transfer your will to Me through My mother, Mary.

5/12/97

Dear Jesus,

I blew it again last night when my self was feeling neglected on Mother's Day and asked ... to honor me. Help me put this needy self aside once and for all and let these slights roll off.

Help!

Dear Ginny,

Help from Me is readily available as you just pause and LISTEN to Me. You have come a long way in not allowing yourself to be pulled into a verbal battle, but you must now expect absolutely nothing from your family. I will fulfill all your needs, Just pray for them. Don't try to change them. Only I can do this when and if they choose to LISTEN. Relax. Listen to soothing music. Love others for Me, Ginny.

5/13/97

Dear Jesus,

It seems so much simpler to leave it all to You in prayer. Please give me this gift of self control.

Dear Ginny,

When you deliver yourself, your needs and your problems to Me in prayer, I am always willing to carry the burden with you. I do not say that I will deliver you from it or from the circumstances, but will assist you in the daily cross so that you will continue to live in My Will.

My Will, as you read earlier today, is always known to you, if you but LISTEN to Me. Leave <u>all</u> the discipline of others to Me. LISTEN as I work on you. LISTEN to others, then, refer them to Me for guidance.

I love you. I have always loved you.

5/14/97Dear Jesus,

Your message today is so right on. A short while ago, in my prayer, You inspired me to call a lady whom I saw at Mass. In Your humor, she just came here. Wow!

Dear Ginny,

I love to speak with you in many and varied ways. You are finally hearing Me in many of My ways, but, with time, you will hear Me more in other ways. Thank you for LISTENING and responding as best as you can at the moment. More refining is necessary. Just rest in Me and I'll do the work. Imagine yourself on a cloud or in a chariot with Me driving and also sitting beside you.

5/21/97

Dear Jesus,

... said I needed to ask You what I needed to have answered. Please help me.

Dear Ginny,

Almost always you think you want to do My will and then you run off and do your own thing. At some time, when you are LISTENING carefully and not distracted with a myriad of chores etc., I will answer this deep question.

As you rest in Me and trust more in Me, you will be more ready and willing and able to deal with what I must tell you. In the meantime, relax and LISTEN to Me.

Your loving Lord and Master, Jesus the Christ

5/31/97

Dear Jesus,

I haven't been sleeping all that well lately. Do You want me to continue looking for medications or are You asking me to spend more time with You? If so, please help me use this time properly.

Dear Ginny,

I am not adverse to your looking for ways to combat your sleep problem. I do want you to use this and any other problem as a means to get closer to Me. As you search for a medical answer, continue to try to meditate. I will teach you to advance one step at a time.

You have been LISTENING more to Me when I send My heat to stop you in your tracks. Begin to sense other more subtle ways of My connection to you. In this peace and security, you will come more and more to rely on Me and My mother.

I love you, Ginny

Go in peace, Jesus

6/11/97

Dear Jesus,

Thank you for defining peace as loving faith at rest. Today it seemed that I had a long way to go to reach this peace, but the ladies comforted me in Your name and I feel much calmer.

Dear Ginny,

My peace does pass all understanding. You are not alone in your trials. I am always with you, and I alone can give you a sense of security in the midst of any problem. Come to Me directly and ask of Me. I am always available to LISTEN. I may not reply to you immediately in a way that will seem to satisfy, but I will always give you the strength to endure. Trials come and go. With each one you become stronger and more agile and more aware of My Presence. I ask a lot of you because I love you and want you to

become more perfected in My Love.

6/19/97

Dear Jesus.

How wonderful it feels to want to do Your will. I feel an excitement inside I haven't felt in years. Please help me to pause before I go off on a tangent doing my will.

Dear Ginny,

Abide, obey, bear fruit. Live in the moment. Rest in My Love and you will be at peace. LISTEN to your heart and the promptings of My Holy Spirit. If what I seem to ask seems confusing, and it doesn't apply for all the tenets of discernment, wait a bit longer for confirmation. Expect that you will be attacked. Be aware when this happens. Be alert to all around you in a gentle but firm way. Live in My Love and you will find My peace which the world cannot give, and even tries to take from you.

6/27/97

Dear Jesus,

What happens when people think I am overwhelming? Is it in me or is it something in them?

Dear Ginny,

Be alert to the body language and facial expressions of those with whom you are speaking. If you sense that they are not attending to what you are trying to communicate, or if they seem agitated by something you are saying, STOP. If they are not interested in LISTENING they are not interested in hearing even if what is being said is extremely profound. Be a lady and don't force yourself on anyone. Remember I am a gentleman and always await an invitation.

6/30/97

Dear Jesus,

Thank you for being God and teaching me who I am in You. I truly want ot do Your will and reach what You have in store for me.

Dear Ginny,

Relax, rest, refrain from criticism. LISTEN to your heart, bear your crosses with dignity, recognize the good in all others, free yourself from self defacing thoughts and actions. You can and will succeed in the ministry I have in store for you if you continue to LISTEN and obey Me.

You can already see the fruits of abiding in Me and obeying My commands. Even your problems have a way of blessing you.

I love your openness and your defense of My truth.

7/19/97

Dear Jesus,

Today will be my sixth annual visit to the campfire at the Little House of Prayer. I know that You and Mary have visited there often. If it be Your will, allow us a supernatural happening so that we not be thought crazy and that unbelievers may believe.

Dear Ginny,

You have already received your gift from Me last evening -the poem- as you sat before Me in My Blessed Sacrament

Go open and expectant but don't be disappointed if you see nothing. I will be there and will touch hardened hearts and reveal Myself in a quiet way to many.

Be available to LISTEN and to put your arm around any who would need to see My Love in a real way.

I love you, Your dear Jesus

Poem 7/18/97

I reach out and touch you

Be open

I reach out and touch you

Be holy

I reach out and touch you

Be careful and caring

I reach out and touch you

Be loving

I reach out and touch you

Be My Beloved

I reach out and touch you

Be pure

I reach out and touch you

and tell you I love you

and ask you to

always be Mine

7/31/97

Dear Jesus,

What do You will from me?

Dear Ginny,

I ask for an open and willing heart prepared to LISTEN and act on what I say. I ask for fervent prayers directed towards those whom I send to you as requests. I ask for a spirit of praise and thanksgiving and a heart ready and willing to obey. I ask for thoughts centered solely on Me and on My Will. I ask for a gentle voice and a gentle spirit directed inwards towards loving and respecting Ginny and outwards toward all. I ask for sincerity and honesty and love and peace and perseverance and hope. I ask for total surrender to Me and My mother with the assistance of your personal, available guardian angel.

8/13/97

Dear Ginny,

As you sit before MY Tabernacle, be aware of My Presence and My Love. Allow yourself the time to sit still so that My peace may penetrate to the very depths of your being.

Realize the privilege you have to be able to come here as often as you do and find Me here just waiting patiently.

When others find you waiting patiently both here and at your home, they will begin to see the newer you.

Continue to LISTEN to My call and act on it.

You know what happens when you over do. When you do My Will with joy, you may be tired, but also refreshed in spirit.

8/24/97

Dear Jesus,

As I read that meekness is the cure for bitterness, I ask that you show me ways I may act this way and not be a doormat, but a child of Yours.

Dear Ginny,

Humility is the virtue most seen in My mother, Mary. She never put herself in the center or spent time reprimanding others. She was silent and in prayer doing MY Will.

When you have to have your way in things, or need to be understood, you are not being humble. Humility lets the other have the last word–right or wrong–and lets the other sit in or on his or her own behavior.

Be hasty to apologize rather than criticize. Be careful of the tender feelings of the other.

Rest in Me. Relax. LISTEN to My voice. Respond, don't react. Love.

Love, Jesus

9/4/97

Dear Jesus,

Thank you for all the "chance" encounters to speak with others of what you are doing in our lives.

Dear Ginny,

What a change to have you looking

optimistically rather than in the pessimistic way you used to behave.

Since following Me with a more sincere heart and will, the changes have been encouraging.

Keep on thinking of others ahead of yourself and continue in your search for spending more time LISTENING and encouraging others rather than talking of yourself. This is an area in which further improvement would be desirable.

Speak of Me often in love. Guard your heart, but don't isolate it. Be vulnerable, but not so open you are seriously hurt. I am with you.

9/9/97

Dear Jesus,

Thank you once again for bringing my sin to mind. I appreciate the grace you give me to write another note of apology. I'm exhausted from the spiritually busy day I've had.

Dear Ginny,

I appreciate your LISTENING to ... today. As you LISTENED you were also the recipient of her affirming you by calling you by name regularly.

Tonight you will sleep well and be available to learn more of Me tomorrow. Be waiting to apply what I teach. Recall your impatience ... .

You recognized it and I rewarded you by allowing you to be aware of her visual handicap. Enjoy the game.

9/11/97

Dear Jesus,

Thank you for bringing me on this retreat. I can see more clearly now how I have not been silent and how all these noises keep me from hearing You more often and more clearly.

Dear Ginny,

These silences in regard to Me can be likened to keeping the wax from building up in your ears. When it is building, My voice is muffled; when it is impacted My voice is silenced within you. Keep the wax from building by learning to apply the lessons you have learned on silence. When you have heard all twelve areas, you will be amazed at the progress you have already made in removing the wax. Much more needs work, but you are well on your way to hearing Me more clearly and more often.

9/15/97

Dear Jesus,

After learning last week of the twelve facets of silence, I realize that all of these areas need to be in balance so I can better rest in You. Help me to find this balance.

Dearest Ginny,

Sometimes you are trying so hard to rest that you weary both yourself and Me.

LISTEN quietly and attentively in your heart for My Words to you. Still your imagination. Quiet your emotions. Know that I love you deeply. Stop trying to find rest and peace. Just do it.

When you are in a conversation, stop jumping ahead. Stay in the moment and learn what it has to say. LISTEN this morning and only comment when you are invited to offer your opinion. If you stay focused, you will know what I want to happen. Be loving. Be kind. Be sincere.

I love you, Ginny

9/20/97

Dear Ginny,

I am all goodness. I desire only the best for you and for all your family-for everyone. When unhappiness besets you, I am there in the midst of it. Continue as you have been trying to do to look for Me in the midst of all.

Trust has been violated by many in their actions towards you. I can always be trusted. Don't look back at these situations; look forward to new encounters in My name.

Take the edge off your voice when you are giving criticism. Blend it with praise. It will sound much better and be more LISTENED to by the other.

Love all. Be careful to say what I will, not what you think.

9/26/97

Dear Jesus,

I have generally come on strong rather than gently. Help me to be more gentle.

Dear Ginny,

Once again you have come closer to me in the Sacrament of Reconciliation. It pleases Me when souls desiring to come closer to Me take advantage of this sacrament. True humility is necessary. As you continue to confess frequently, I will be able to speak more clearly and distinctly to you through the vehicle of the priest. He is My vicar on earth. Pray for priests. Love them. See Me in them and others. Be loving. Be caring.

10/2/97

Dear Jesus,

I need reminding often about meekness. I have not yet really understood on a deep level what it means.

My dear Ginny,

Completely turn your will over to Me and you will always be acting in meekness. You will be able to see My way and the others will not feel overwhelmed.

Meekness is relying on Me for guidance and then following through on My requests. Do your own thing and all havoc will break loose. Others will see a change. They may not like the change because your change may not allow them to continue on their path of destruction.

Don't waver. Applause from others has no significance in My greater plan.

Heaven is your goal. Don't waver. LISTEN even more closely to My guiding.

Love to you, Jesus and the Father

10/7/97

Dear Jesus,

As I said on waking this morning I still talk too much about ... . I react too quickly ... .Help me change.

Dear Ginny,

Once again in the past you would not

have recognized these character defects. It will become easier to overcome as you appropriate My grace more. As you know many of the saints had continuous struggles with their flaws.

As you enter the day today, offer to pray with ... so that both of you bring Me into the situation. Call on Me as often as you have the need. I am here beside you and within you. Don't disturb My peace with agitation. Let Me be the one to lead the conversation. Actively Listen, but don't offer advice unless I specifically nudge you. All will be well. I love you both.

Your friend and lover, Jesus

10/10/97

Dearest Ginny,

As you read more of supernatural happenings to others, you realize that I am really present to those who are willing to let themselves go forward and LISTEN to Me. Recognize that I know all and can see all. I allow you to be available to My Will, but you are free to choose your own way as you often do.

Love others as I love you. Take the time to LISTEN to them and speak of My Love for you and for them. Let them see Me, not you, so that they know that they don't have to come to you but can come directly to Me.

Lately you have done much better in getting out of the middle once you have helped with the introductions. This please Me.

10/12/97

My dear little Ginny,

I am delighted to continue our conversations. At some time in the future you will be able to remember whatever I say without always writing. Humble yourself. Allow them to have the last word. Keep on coming to Me with your sorrows and concerns and also your joys and surprises. Look to Me for help whenever and wherever.

Speak to ... about what is happening in your spiritual life. He will direct you as to what to do about your guardian angel. He will help you now that he has recovered and you have already shown growth in the life of the Spirit.

Remember to LISTEN and follow his counsel. Be open to his direction. Pray and love and LISTEN and learn. I love you as I love all My children. Love does not diminish.

10/14/97

Dear Jesus,

Yesterday I tried to help someone. I thought I was doing it in Your name. Can you help me with discernment?. I'm uneasy.

Dear Ginny,

Discernment is yours for the asking. This person is not someone whom you can help other than by offering her some of your time. She has many others to whom she has gone and can go for help. Continue to pray for her. Offer her kindness and gentleness. Take care of yourself, however, so that you will not be over stretched and unavailable for prayer when I ask.

Be aware that I don't send everyone to you for spiritual help. They would over burden you. Let Me lead you with inner promptings. LISTEN to your heart and your gut. Believe on Me.

11/10/97

Dearest Ginny,

Once again you have come here drawn by My Love. I will show you more each day how to represent this love to others. Balance is necessary in all states of life. When you are out of balance it shows in your demeanor and in your countenance.

Presently you are in a state that is nearly balanced as you have just been reconciled to Me in confession.

Continue to strive for holiness as you continue to LISTEN and to follow Me more closely.

All will come to the ends I have designed when you follow the pattern or path I have given to you. When you love it shows on your face. Work with Me. Be on My team always. Follow My rules and you will not need to sit on the bench. I love you, Ginny

11/19/97

Dear Jesus,

Presently there seems to be confusion in my life...a lot of free time. Are you asking me to be in prayer more or in volunteer work, what?

My dear Ginny,

In the stillness, I will speak to your heart. I will speak through others and in sermons. Don't have any plans which can't be rearranged and I will show you My plan. Put some order and structure in your day, but be flexible. Wait for a while on a commitment to a permanent volunteer position.

I speak more in silence, but I speak also in the hubub of the world. Be available. See Me in others. LISTEN more to them and talk less. Follow My lead and My inspirations and the path will already be trodden down. You can do My will not My work.

I've already done My work.

11/22/97

Dear Jesus,

I think I have such zeal for You and I'm even crying now that nobody seems to care. Please help me to learn ,or how to direct this zeal.

Dear Ginny,

Today's people do not want to hear of heaven, hell, judgment or sin. They want only to LISTEN to the wonders around them. Continue to do as I have been directing you lately and go to those who will LISTEN. Often there are those who are eaves dropping and will hear something about Me which will stimulate to prayer or reading or Scripture or to reconciliation. Your van is a tangible sign of your witness. Continue to hang on to Me tightly and you will not be pulled away by the tide of public opinion or detraction towards you. I am with you. You can count on Me.

11/29/97

Dear God,

When I am in the monastery it usually seems easy to be close to You. When I go outside, I often forget to call on You. Please help.

Dearest Ginny,

Consciously think of Me whenever you begin a new task, a phone call, visit, or whatever. As I have asked you before on several occasions, pause, then pray, then go on in MY direction. This pause, now connected to your prayer, will give you the necessary time to check in with Me before you step off a cliff. I have been giving you inspiration during your phone conversations. Sometimes you LISTEN when I ask you to wait and other times you just continue and end up gossiping. Be more careful and prudent and gentle and refined and loving and silent. I am not heard in the noise and din. Love Me.

I love you, God the Father

12/1/97

Dear Jesus,

I recognize once again that I am not as gentle and compassionate as you would have me. Show me how, please.

Dearest Ginny,

LISTEN more carefully when others are speaking to you. Don't butt in.

Respond in a caring manner. Speak with Me and ask Me what I would have you say and do. I am responsible for all My children. You may not have to do anything but LISTEN to them and to Me. You are not responsible for being the answer to everyone's prayer. That is My duty. Relax and be ready and available to LISTEN. I will guide you in how to assist gently. Go forth in peace.

12/2/97

My dear Ginny,

As you have just read I am disappointed as I know what you are capable of accomplishing for Me. The more open and receptive you are to My call, the more willing you are to be a silent LISTENER, the more I am able to fulfill My plan through you.

Keep the lines of communication open. Let go of your worldly cares and concerns. Be available to Me at a moment's notice. LISTEN to My word. Be discerning and I will call on you more frequently. Keep all avenues open to Me. Be wary of the enemy's intrusion. Call on Me for protection, but be always available, on call, and ready to act or pray.

12/7/97

Dear Ginny,

When you are in sync with Me, you are able to hear My whisperings to your soul.

It is fine with Me that you now look forward to time away from others to spend with Me. You are not hiding, but learning to come closer to Me. You are realizing more how little value the things of the world have, if their end is not directed to Me. There is nothing wrong with people wanting to have fun and relaxation. At this time, as you are trying to grow closer to Me, it is wise for you to spend more time with Me, and less and less in the world.

I allow you to feel the tension. When you discern discomfort I am speaking to you. LISTEN and respond.

12/8/97

My dearest Ginny,

Thank you for coming here today on My mother's feat day to ask Me what My will is for you.

My will is for you to do My work here where I have placed you. Each day I have something I desire of you if and when you are open to Me. Sometimes you will be aware of what I am asking. At other times, you will have no idea what is happening. Please LISTEN. I open your ears and your heart to hear My call and also to hear the cry of My people. Don't let them call in vain. Be there for them. Don't count the cost. Eternity is at stake. Believe, love, admire, work, pray and most of all obey Me.

Your Lord Jesus

12/13/97

After communion I felt Jesus say that I should act as if I were blind folded, take His hand, and He would lead me through a maze or a mine field. He alone knows the destination. If I am attached to family or friends, the group becomes unmanageable and someone will be badly hurt. Jesus alone knows the way and is with everyone of them.

Whenever you come to Me in prayer I

am there LISTENING because I am already with you. Continue on your way of trying to make your life a prayer so that the connection with Me is always on. If you keep the line open with Me there will not need to be a pause in our dialogue. Turn everything over to Me. Keep an open heart to Me. Refrain from sin or its occasion. Love, Love, Love. Forgive all and the communication will be fruitful.

I love you darling, Ginny, Jesus

12/14/97

Dear Ginny,

As I speak with and to you, you are

becoming more and more aware of My presence with you. Invite Me into everything you do.

Keep on keeping on. Invite Me regularly to be the life within you so that you come to the realization that I am always with you. Become more aware of how delighted I am when you LISTEN to My voice and heed My call.

Visit Me often. Tell Me all your cares and your woes and your sorrows and let Me sift them through My gentle fingers and hands of infinite and everlasting love.

Be loving to all you meet as you are meeting Me in others.

12/15/97

If you heed My words and follow them, you are on the path that will lead you to eternity in My kingdom. If you do not LISTEN to My voice, you are on the road to destruction. The choice is yours. I endowed you with free will and will not grab it away from you. You must daily offer your will to Me.

Forget all the heartaches and distresses you are dealing with. Concentrate only on doing My will. Forgive all those who have distressed you and offer your prayers for them and their salvation.

Don't try to follow the path or pattern I have drawn for anyone else. Your plan is unique. Stop. LISTEN. Play. Rest. Work. Be alive and available and I will accomplish My plan through you.

12/18/97

Dear Jesus,

Thank you for helping me be gracious and thankful yesterday. I was able to see some of the growth in Ginny.

Dearest Ginny,

Until you die, you will be growing. It is up to you how much and to what extent. As you LISTEN to Me and follow My lead, you will become stronger in a more gentle way. It will not be necessary for you to be forceful in sharing your values and your beliefs. They will become even more a part of you-so much of you that, just your being, not doing, will alert others. You will still be misunderstood and perhaps ridiculed at times by others; but so was I.

Keep focused and aware of My intervention in your thought life and especially in your spoken life.

Be still (not silent) and know that I am God.

12/28/97

Dear Lord,

I sense that You are with me when I feel heat. I believe You are asking me to be aware of Your presence when I feel nothing.

Dearest Ginny,

Feelings can often be wrong because they are changeable. Know that I am with you regardless of how you are feeling. Take My peace, place it in your heart and call on Me. LISTEN to your heart. I have impressed much there already. You need only remember a piece of Scripture, a song, a homily, a story one of My teachings to you and I will become stronger in your awareness.

As you have let go of other persons and things, there is so much more space in your heart and soul and mind for Me and My mother. Honor her.

!2/30/97

Dear Jesus,

I do feel pain when I see others going against Your will. When I try to instruct and admonish, I am shunned. Is prayer the only way You want from me?

My dear little one,

I have been asking you repeatedly for

your prayers and for your will. I do give you the go ahead to speak at times and at other times I ask you to pray. Be sensitive to My leading and you will know what I ask of you. Last night you allowed your hurt feelings to intrude on My will for you in the situation. The other person was not open at the time to receive your correction, especially in the abrupt way in which you presented it. Much of the time it is My desire that you LISTEN to the whole story and respond at a later time when you have researched your answer and can be more objective, I will give you the time to speak and the time to refrain from speaking.

12/31/97

I reach out-reach back in

I offer you My love-give Me your heart

I light up Your soul-bring My light to others

I shower you with graces-share them

I speak to you with gentleness-be tender

I touch your heart-allow it to soften

I Am God-reverence Me

Hold out your hand-I will clasp it

Give Me your concerns-I will carry them

Allow Me to hold you–rest in My arms

Kneel down before Me–I'm all that you need

12/31/97

I kneel before You in adoration

Seeking only to know You more

I reach out to touch You–You answer

You tell me to LISTEN more

LISTEN to the silence

LISTEN to the stillness

LISTEN to the pain

Come often and spend time with Me

Treasure our moments alone

I speak so much more in the silence

I speak so much more in the pain

I come to bring healing and wholeness

I'm there in the grief and the pain

I want to live within you

I want you to always be pure

I love you and want your companionship

I always will be there for you

12/31/97

I reach out-reach back in

I offer you My love-give Me your heart

I light up Your soul-bring My light to others

I shower you with graces-share them

I speak to you with gentleness-be tender

I touch your heart-allow it to soften

I Am God-reverence Me

Hold out your hand-I will clasp it

Give Me your concerns-I will carry them

Allow Me to hold you-rest in My arms

Kneel down before Me-I'm all that

you need

1/17/98

Dear Jesus,

It has become easier to LISTEN more to You and to do Your will. Thank you for this grace.

Dear little one,

Each day as you comply with My graces I shower you with more. Be aware of My love within you and it will become second nature for you and it will become second nature for you to bring this love to all. You will show no favorites. I have no favorites. Some will accept your love for them and others will reject it. This is not your concern. Just love when and where I ask it of you.

Continue to come and visit Me often. Bring your joys and your sorrows and share them with Me. I am all you need. Desire this.

1/23/98

My dear Ginny,

Have no fear that any power comes from you. It is all under My control.

I allow you to use it for ill because you have been given a free will.

Continue to desire to be always in My will. Keep My commandments and LISTEN to My voice. It is soft and melodious. It does not shout and is never going to fill you with fear.

Come closer to Me in a special way. Let all your guard down in My Presence. Allow Me to fill you with My Love.

Be aware of Me. Continue your path of self discovery so that you might give all of your self to Me to do with as I wish.

Keep looking at your areas of sin and defect, I will help you. Call on Me.

I love you Virginia Carol, Jesus

1/31/98

Dear Ginny,

When I call–LISTEN. Wherever I lead–go. I offer you all the grace you need to accomplish whatever I ask of you. This grace becomes available as you proceed, not before. For this you must trust completely in Me.

I call often in the disguise of others. Look hard and you will see Me. Treat all as you would treat Me if I were with you.

Forget yourself.

Be prepared for future sufferings by covering yourself and others in prayer and by living your life consecrated or set apart for Me.

Control your impulses by calling out

and hanging on to Me. Become kinder and more gentle and eternal life will begin here in a spectacular way for you.

2/4/98

My dear one,

Trusting in Me is remembering all I have given to you as examples. Today's example is that of a little girl skipping along blissfully one hand in that of each trusted parent. When a crack appears in the sidewalk, the parents lift up on the child's arms and keep her just up and away from the crack. If a scary dog comes along, the loving Daddy scoops the child up in his arms. The Daddy would not allow the child to stray into a dangerous neighborhood. He might even restrict the child to her room lovingly if she strayed away. He would smother her with his hugs and kisses and then reprimand her for not staying on the path he drew for her.

You are My child. You are presently in a cocoon. I hold you with My hand as does My mother. I enclose you in the cloud of My Love and glory and convey you in MY chariot. What more could you ask? Sit back, relax, LISTEN and learn all I have to teach you. I desire to please you and be pleased by you, My love. Ginny, stop fighting Me.

2/9/98

When prayer comes from the heart, I am the initiator. I am the true initiator of all prayer. LISTEN attentively to My call within and around you and I will lead you into prayer.

The deeper you look into MY eyes and see the pain in the world–the more you will surrender yourself to Me for the benefit of others.

Prayer is speaking to Me in love with the graces I have already offered you. It is responding to Me when I call on you. It is stopping what you are doing to think of Me and then

returning to your chore and
remembering Me.

Prayer pleases Me and My Father. It is supplied to you by the inner yearnings of the Holy Spirit. All of your being needs to be involved in prayer. This is why you

have needed to let go and relax in Me. Be all Mine.

I love you, Ginny, Jesus

3/8/98

Dearest Ginny,

Keep LISTENING. I have much more to speak to the silence of your heart as you allow Me to open it more and more. You will be pleasantly surprised by what will happen in and around you as your heart expands. I will fill you with more of My knowledge and wisdom and love and generosity and compassion and gentleness. Others will see the changes in you. Be certain to tell them of the quiet times you spend alone with Me.

LISTEN as I call you to deeper prayer. This will not require more time in prayer, but a life of prayer which will permeate your entire lifestyle more and more.

I will be refining your exterior as I do your interior. You will be able to reach more people as you recognize how I desire you to respond or initiate conversations about Me with others. Relax. Go in peace. Flow in My Love.

I bless you in My name, Jesus

3/10/98

Dearest Ginny,

When you do not do the good deeds I have prepared for you they go undone. Someone else may be sent at a later time to assist in the task I offered to you. Someone may not. An opportunity has been lost forever. It is your task to LISTEN closely to Me and discern My will.

Presently I am calling you to respond to the article on confession. I will help you with it. Be kind but also be truthful. Be steadfast in upholding the teachings of the Church coming from Scripture and Tradition.

It is My will that people humble themselves to Me in sincere repentance. Humility and humiliation are not the same.

Continue to wave the banner of truth. Carry it yourself. Be willing to die to yourself to do this.

My work today is carried out by soldiers just like you who think they are alone. My army is hidden, but it is sizable.

Pray- Pray-Pray

Love, Jesus

3/12/98

My dear one, Ginny

My Holy Spirit is the One who comes upon you in order for you to LISTEN to Me more often.

Come aside in My Love. Learn that it is My hand you ought to have taken all these many years when you were looking for love in all the wrong places. The fruits of the Holy Spirit are what bring self control. We are the source of this for you. You have expected too much from others when you thought they would want to help you with this lack of control. They were too busy with sorting out their own problems to assist you. It was easier for them to think you were their problem. Pray for all those with problems that they find the solution in Me.

3/24/98

I am with you to fill you with My Love and My peace. Decide for Me. Stop going your own way and sticking yourself into the business of others. Place yourself at My feet and accept My extended hand. I will nourish you forever with My own

Body and Blood. I will teach you from My Word.

Please follow Me and be always willing to hold My hand and go where I lead you.

Be filled with My peace as you LISTEN to My directions. Don't be concerned about details.

Simplify your life. Don't worry about anything, I will be available to you at all times.

Go forward. Be at peace. Rejoice and praise Me. I love all My children. I will open their cocoons at the proper time.

3/28/98

Dear Ginny,

Come even closer and LISTEN to Me.

I respond whenever you ask of Me. Sometimes, as you are aware, the answer is in the negative. Regardless of the answer, I desire your gratitude. Your life should become one of praise and gratitude.

You can never overwhelm Me with your requests, but I see you become overwhelmed yourself with the magnitude of your needs and wants. Because of this, I have pity or compassion on you. Sometimes I invite you to rest again and lay your burdens down. I really desire that you stop before picking them up at all. They are too heavy for you. Pick them up only after I sort through them and hand you the ones I want you to carry. Your load is heavy when you are not waiting for Me to invite you to carry it. When the invitation is Mine, I supply you with everything you need to carry it for My honor and glory.

Love you, Ginny, Jesus

4/16/98

Dear Ginny,

You are not always open to receive My Love and My mercy. You still want to do things your own way.

When I ask you to do something for Me it would suffer you well to pause and ask Me How I would want you to accomplish the task I have asked of you. You will be surprised at the ease when you LISTEN first for directions.

This week you have once again been caught up in a frenzy and a whirlwind of agitation. You have become nervous and over talked instead of LISTENING. Accept My peace and relax. It is necessary for you to be available and relaxed for the long haul, not the short spurt.

I Am Mercy. I Am Love. I Am Wisdom. I Am Holiness. I Am Graciousness. All of these attributes are found in Me because I Am.

5/2/98

My dear Ginny,

Climb up into My lap and let Me hold you as you long to be held. Don't wiggle. Don't squirm. Just relax. Allow yourself to be at peace. Fall asleep. Wake up and find that I am still holding you. Reach up and hug Me and I will hug and hold you. Find peace. I will never leave you nor forsake you. You will not have to look at the clock and think that your time is up. You may get up and walk away, but, when you decide to return, I will he here waiting for you. I will reach down and pick you up again. See how easily I LISTEN and comfort and console. Come now back into My embrace and find refreshment, peace, comfort and solace.

I love you, Jesus and the Father

5/3/98

My dear one, Ginny

LISTEN to Me in the silence. Hear My whispered greeting and love. Find these times alone with Me the source of your greatest strength and consolation.

See how much I love you. I have

invited you to walk along with Me and My mother, Mary. You thought you had experienced your Garden time with Me when going through your own trials. As you know, this pain of ... is causing you much more pain. I am here for you. I am here for all of you. Rely on Me and be at peace.

Love, Jesus

I am in control of all.

5/6/98

Dear one, Ginny

Yesterday you allowed yourself to get off track. See how easily this happens. Your voice was raised and filled with tension and anger. I was not pleased. You have been given much. Much is to be expected of you.

Be more careful. Be more aware of any dangers coming towards you. Find your solace in Me. None of your talking is going to solve the problem. First of all, the problem is ..., not yours. Once again I remind you that your part is that of prayer, of LISTENING, and of being of such practical help as you are invited to be.

Stop comparing your problem..No two problems are ever the same, so no two solutions are either. Each problem is like a snowflake–unique. Only I have the answer. Pray.

Love, Jesus

5/7/98

I come to you under the form of Bread and Wine–to give My life for you to share with others.

I come to you disguised.

I come to you in silence.

I come to you filled with love.

Bring this love to others.

LISTEN to them in silence.

Tell them of My love for you.

Share the power of My Word.

I come to you in the quiet of your heart.

You will recognize Me most when you are quiet of heart.

When you are agitated and confused, you are unable to sort out My voice.

Peace and tranquility are My gifts to you.

Continue to pray for them.

Store all the memories of this peace.

Call on them and on Me whenever you are disturbed.

I come to you Body and Blood, Soul and Divinity.

I come to share My life with you.

I come because I love you.

Share My Love.

Be My love to others.

Eternal life is now and forever.

Cherish it.

I love you, Ginny, Jesus

5/13/98

My dear Ginny,

I instructed you last year to abide, obey and bear fruit.

The fruit is beginning. Because you have obeyed you are showing results in the fruit of the Spirit. This is a life long process. It does not happen over night and will not continue unless you continue to allow yourself to be fertilized and pruned and sometimes transplanted. You must continue to abide in My Word. Be saturated with it. Live the works of mercy and the fruits will grow.

In heaven the fruit is plentiful. It can be plentiful here on earth when My people LISTEN and heed Me.

Continue in your love, Jesus

5/22/98

Dear Ginny,

I hear you cry and I LISTEN. I ask you to partake of My suffering-you agree and then you cry.

Know that I hear you and feel your pain. Hold tight to Me and My Love. I will be with you through all your trials when you ask.

Stop running out in front where you are more vulnerable to the enemy. Pause. Reflect. It only takes a moment, but will save so much in the future.

Act only on My direction. Otherwise be still and wait and calm down. Shed your tears for Me and others. Don't waste them on self pity.

6/1/98

Dear Ginny,

Trust Me to know what is best for you. Allow Me to be in control. Praise and thank Me even in the seemingly bad times. I can always make lemonade with your lemons. Relax and rest in My peace. Lay your burdens down.

I come to you whenever you call. Wherever you are. Thank you for taking time away from all else to sit here before My Tabernacle. I alone know the outcome of your circumstances. LISTEN to My voice. Hear and heed My call. Bring My

Love to others. Expect rejection. Some of them rejected Me.

Is it not safe to say that they will also reject you?

Focus yourself on Me and on changing your own life. It is far from perfect and can do with much refining. I am with you. I love you. I hear and I answer you.

Go in peace.

6/11/98

Dear Ginny,

Keep focused on Me. Pray for those who hurt you and others. Believe in Me and My Word.

Live your life in purity of heart in your thoughts, in words and in deeds.

Follow My lead. Be docile in My hands. Be alert for the enemy who is out to catch you when you let your guard down. Do not be concerned about being thought crazy. So was I. Never let go of My hand. I will keep you from destruction. I will lead you in the way of truth. I will give you discernment-if you would but LISTEN closely to Me.

Bind yourself to My cross. Know that you cannot experience anything without My knowledge or consent. Call on Me in your pain. I will answer. I am here for you, Hang on tight,

6/13/98

Dearest Ginny,

An experience in the desert is not a punishment. In the desert, you must lean on Me and not in your own understanding. It is dry in the desert. Food and drink are sparse if available at all. Focus must be on Me or on the circumstances. One can learn much during this time.

Since there is no entertainment available one is more readily available to LISTEN to and respond to Me.

Make the most of your circumstances. Look for Me in all of them. I may come as the sole rider. Do not be fearful. Do not try to hide from me. I will search you out. I would rather have you come out and sup with Me and keep Me company. I am your peace and your salvation.

6/26/98

My Ginny,

None of those I chose to do My will and My work were perfect. I choose whomever I desire for the task at hand. I give opportunities, I invite again, I offer the means to perform the task , and still many do not praise Me.

LISTEN closely to My call. Remember that you are not and will not be perfect before I use you. Act in humility, knowing this. Know also that others are not perfect. Free them from your unnecessary criticism and allow them to grow.

I do much of My refining in the dark and bleak. Most people are more in touch with Me at these times than they are in their extreme happiness, wealth, power and self respect.

John the Baptist was in the desert as were Moses and his people. Jonah was in the whale. Relax and learn from your dry and seemingly barren time

6/30/98

I have come to give you life in abundance, All your trials and all your treasured times are known by Me. I see all. I know all. I ask you to do My will. I hold you accountable to Me in this regard. Whenever I give you a gift, it is to be opened and used by you for the advancement of My work and My kingdom. It is not to be hoarded, but shared.

As you already know, any gifts which are not used are redistributed for the benefit of all.

I am teaching you to share. I am teaching you to LISTEN and to be gentle and compassionate. I am opening up the words of Scripture to you in a new way. I am preparing you for a specific task. Be alert. Be on guard. Be ready to come when I call and go where I send you, Ginny.

7/1/98

Go forth and do My work which is My will for you. LISTEN closely. I asked you to fast, instead you over ate and became ill.

When will you LISTEN and OBEY? Don't be so concerned about the how's and why's, just LISTEN and OBEY. I speak to you before you over eat and give you the opportunity to sacrifice, but you don't understand, so you disobey. Ask Me for release from your gluttony and I will answer you. Your job is simply to LISTEN and OBEY What could be simpler? (Lord, I ask you now to remove this demon of gluttony, and I thank you for answering me.)

Be at peace, My child. Acknowledge My Love and concern for you. Go in peace to love others.

7/3/98

As you continue to come and LISTEN to Me even in the dry times, I will minister to you. I will give you peace and serenity despite the circumstances around you.

Be My peace maker. Light My way with the inner light of My Love shining forth from you. Share this love with others. Do not be concerned about a response. Just continue to love and to pray. Use the personality I have given you. Don't abuse it.

Go visit ... and give her My Love. Follow your heart when you have placed it in Mine. Enjoy the day.

7/7/98

I send the sun to warm you

I send the rain to cleanse you

I send pain to save you

I send the moon to light your dark paths

I send suffering to test your love

I send My Son to hold your hand

I send you to bring Me to others

LISTEN to Me

Learn from Me

I ask your obedience to My Will for you

7/13/98

Dear Ginny,

ON your own you are nothing and can do nothing. I am your Creator and Sustainer even if I am not Lord of your life. You cannot blink or take your next breath without Me.

I understand your present frustrations. You frustrate Me in this way all the time. You pour out your pain to Me and to others and we offer suggestions, you almost immediately refuse them although you are improving in this area.

You will not be able to help all those who cry on your shoulder. Some of them do not want help at the moment. LISTEN. Speak to them on Me then move out or on. Shake the dust. As you had to become broken before you could be refashioned, so do others. Do not blame yourself for not being able to do something because even I am not fully a part of your life or those whom you would try to help. Relax. Take a deep breath. Put the problems of the past two days behind you. Remember the beauty and the change in you.

7/14/98

Dear one, Ginny

Ignorance of the truth does not totally free you from sin's penalty and the need to confess. It is your solemn obligation to learn about the truth. When you were not aware of some facets of the truth, I enlightened your mind and your will as in the feelings you often had in regard to your children & teaching. You are responsible for heeding the messages I give deep within you.

Continue to LISTEN to My instructions and My correction. I am with you and desire you to be all that I have created you to be. Let go of all that is not of Me or will not bring you or others closer to Me.

Be in the world. I created it. I desire that you enjoy it. Do not be a part of this world , but a part of Eternity which began in you at Baptism.

7/15/98

LISTEN as I speak to you. LISTEN with your entire being, but LISTEN especially with your heart.

LISTEN as others speak to you. LISTEN with a heart flooded with My love and kindness and compassion because you have LISTENED to Me before and because you continue to LISTEN to Me while LISTENING to the other.

As you become even more focused on Me this will become easier for you to do. As you LISTEN to Me, you must also OBEY.

I speak into your heart; I speak in your pain; I speak in your circumstances and in the beauty of nature and of those who are around you.

Continue to pray for those who are in pain and especially for those who seem to cause you pain. Turn them and the pain over to Me immediately in prayer and move on. Don't stand still.

I love you, Ginny

Yours, Jesus

7/30/98

Dear Ginny,

As I lay down My life you must be willing to do likewise. I did the Father's Will, so must you.

Laying down your life is a gift. The gift is given ultimately to Me. If I ask you to lay down your life you will not necessarily be rewarded by those who are the recipients. I will reward you in the hereafter. I lay down My life at the right time, not willy nilly. Wait, poised for Me to give the signal. Do not continue to be gullible and become over tired for trivialities.

LISTEN closely to Me. I speak in the silence of your heart. I am pleased with your progress. Much still needs to be done.

Be patient. Be calm. Be watchful in expectation of My call. Be discerning. Be gentle. Be humble. Be aware. Be loving.

Stay close to Me and My mother.

8/5/98

My dear Ginny,

As you continue to acknowledge your sins and failings, you continue to grow in love towards Me.

LISTEN when I speak. My mercy precedes your actions. I will invite you to discontinue your thoughts before you put them into action.

You saw this morning how Father paused during the disturbance of noise. This will not be easy for you, but My help will be with you and the reward is an eternity with Me.

Leave all your problems with Me. Change your way of relating to others. LISTEN to their prattle and their problems. Allow Me to give you insight and then share with them when I ask. As you relax and become more interested in others, they will be more interested in learning of Me from you. Mercy is yours for the asking,

8/8/98

Dear Ginny,

After the resurrection, I returned to My apostles to commission them. I had instructed them prior to the crucifixion, but they were somewhat overwhelmed by all that I said. They were all ordinary men of the day and were not fully aware of all that I was saying to them. When I breathed My breath–the breath of God–on them, they were filled with the Holy

Spirit and only then fully able to go forth in My name to preach, teach and to sanctify. Only then were they able to do My will. You also can do My will and that of My Father in great things when you continue to be filled with My Spirit-LISTEN to My Word and My will, appropriate it and act on it in love.

8/17/98

Dear Ginny,

A time of exile is often a time of softening of the heart. During trials and tribulations you heart will either harden to keep out everything and everyone including Me-or it will soften so that I can mold it for you.

Pain and suffering and hardship cause different reactions from different people. Stay in My Word-LISTEN to My voice-harden not your heart as in the day of Meribah.

A soft heart will stop hurting after a while. Softness cannot be broken. I have already died for all the evil in the world. Please be willing to suffer along with others for Me.

I am not calling you to be a doormat, but I am calling you to let go of all anger and bitterness and thoughts of revenge. Do what is necessary, but do it with love for yourself and for the other. Justice is a part of mercy.

9/2/98

Dearest Virginia Carol,

As your dear Daddy portrayed you as a singing infant in the nursery you were encouraged to either speak or to be silent. You were never taught and didn't teach, the benefits of LISTENING.

LISTEN. LISTEN to Me. LISTEN to others. Hear their pain as well as feel it. In the speaking, many are able to unburden themselves. It is not at all your task to solve their problems or carry their pain. Simply LISTEN.

When I want to speak to you, I must first get your attention. Be on the alert to hear Me.

When your ear was blocked, I showed

you how to pay more attention. Stop doing so many things at once. There is no hurry. You are not busy as you once were. Relax. Take a deep breath. Enjoy yourself. LISTEN to others attentively and they will be more relaxed in your presence. Speak when I direct you. Take time for pauses. Give Me the credit for the graces you have received. Many will be blessed. You will be rewarded with much inner peace.

9/3/98

Dear Virginia,

I have already died to save you so there should be no fear that I will ever leave you.

Abiding in Me could be likened to floating in a warm sea in a life jacket. Storms will come, but I will be there to sustain you. You can do nothing for yourself. Just lay back and relax and LISTEN quietly for My instruction. Other images I have given you before are that of a cloud and chariot or a roller coaster. In none of these places is there anything you can do but relax and put all your trust in Me. I do not promise freedom from trials or tribulations, pain or death. I do promise life everlasting if you simply abide, obey, and bear fruit. I supply the energy. I give the support. I do the real work. Please follow My instructions. Be at peace.

9/8/98

My Ginny,

There is so much joy in giving. Those who are unable to give cannot fathom this joy. Whenever you are beginning to suffer from your self pity, I will suggest to whom and what you might give. Sometimes you may simply give a smile or a warm hello or a phone call or a hug. In giving, when you are beginning to think and feel that you are running on empty, I will refill or refuel or refresh you.

There will never come a time when you are unable to give something. Know that I am with you. Expect me to LISTEN to your calls. I expect you to LISTEN to Me when I whisper to you. Be alert for My call.

9/11/98

Dear Ginny,

When you come and follow Me, I make two promises to you. I promise you eternal life and I promise you a cross. Both these are connected. It is impossible to have one without the other. Redemptive suffering leads you towards this eternal life. You can either joy in this suffering or waste your time in self pity and lose the value of it.

I have been inviting you to come and follow Me since you were a child. At times you heard Me and did what I asked. I have continued to call and you are now more aware of My call. LISTEN carefully. You now have no distractions for this short period of time. Benefit from all I have to teach you in love.

9/12/98

Dear Virginia,

Without distractions, you are free to learn how to follow Me. After this teaching you will know how to follow and how to LISTEN even in the midst of any distraction. You will know how to be alone with Me even in a crowd. You are already practicing when in a group. More will come as you put yourself aside for Me

Be tender hearted. Be pure. Be holy. Be without spot or blemish. LISTEN to Me and you will not sin. You will have no regrets.

As with any disciple or any athlete, I am teaching you more than you will need to share at any given time. I am testing you to the maximum of your strength so you will go the full way or distance and not grow weary or give up the fight of faith, Be gentle.

9/16/98

Dear one Virginia,

When I begin to speak to the heart of one of My disciples, they are often not aware that it is I. It is a time of discernment and of accountability. If I would use the individual as a prophet there needs to be someone else who can validate My Word. Samuel had Elias. ... is assisting you in your discernment.

When you are used to hearing Me speak to you as you are now-you will need to use the discernment I have given you. In the time ahead, I may speak words for others that you will find difficult to deliver. They must be delivered in love. They may not be received. This is not your fault. They didn't LISTEN to Me either. Do My will. Your reward is eternal life and inner peace.

Love, Jesus,

9/29/98

Dear Ginny,

When I called, Samuel was willing to LISTEN even before he knew it was I.

Be waiting for My call. Be waiting for My further invitation. Because I have invited you to follow , this means I am to lead. I go before you always. Come, follow Me and I will give you rest. There can be no rest found in the things of the world if you first fo not have Me. All is restless. This is not necessarily a physical restlessness but a spiritual one—a constant looking for something or someone to satisfy. You already know I am all you need. Just put this into practice and trust Me with your life.

Love, Jesus

10/6/98

Dearest Virginia.

Once up a time there were two sisters who loved Me and each other. Each gave what she had to give. Martha was a good cook; we were hungry. Mary wasn't as handy in the kitchen as she had not learned this from her mother or the servants, and being at home didn't interest her.

She was interested in LISTENING to Me as were the men. Martha was somewhat jealous as all she needed to do was ask and Mary would have assisted her. Martha wanted to LISTEN, but was afraid of being too forward. She was finding it too important to do all the details herself. She wanted approval.

There is a time in your life to be busy and a time to pause at My feet and soak in My Love. Become more and more like Mary. Being Martha is easy for you.

Love, Jesus

10/7/98

Dearest Virginia,

You have been connected to Me since your Baptism. As you have grown closer to Me this connection has grown stronger. When you sin, the connection weakens. I am always the same; you have changed for better or for worse.

Keep your hand and your heart in Mine. As I prune you, I heal you.

Come closer. LISTEN to all I have to say. Invite Me to be a part of all you do. Be ever more conscious and aware of My Presence.

I desire to be all to you. Lighten your load. Free yourself from all that is unnecessary. Stop repeating your problems. Share them with Me-learn your lesson-and move forward. You will take much longer to reach your destination if, like Tootle, you keep going off track. Red flags are waving. Pay attention to them. Focus on Me.

I love you, darling one.

10/8/98

Dearest Virginia,

Service is the identifying mark of a Christian. I gave My life to serve you. Istill do. I invite you to do likewise.

Stop wanting to be important. This is of no import in My heavenly kingdom. Do My will and that of My

Father. I do not desire that you serve everyone. Speak and LISTEN to Me. I will let you know when and where and how to serve. The world is aware of your availability and wants to see you fill up your hours. They see you as lonely. I see you as My child and I long to have you in communion with Me at all times. This does not mean that you are to become a recluse. I mean to use you for My work in the world. You must continue in training with Me. ..Our walk together will be exciting as you see others come to know Me better.

10/20/98

Dear one, Ginny

I have set you apart as an apostle of these times to bring My message to all who will LISTEN. I have been purifying you of yourself and all that stands in the way of others seeing Me, not you.

I have you studying My Word to know more about Me. I am in relationship with you so that you will know Me in a more direct and intimate way. I have been giving you insights into My Word which you did not have before.

My hand has been on you, protecting you all these years. I have graced you with an ability of knowing right from wrong in a very strong way. I have shown you My truth. I have kept you from sin as long as you have connected with Me. I love you.

10/22/98

Dear Ginny,

As far as it is possible, be at peace with all people. It is not possible with all people in all circumstances. Peace is not the total absence of conflict. Peace is negotiating the conflict in ways which are pleasing to Me. It is absolutely not permissible to ever compromise the truth. Share the truth in love. Share it again. Don't argue. Simply state your case and then stand on it.

Do you expect everyone to agree with you even on the truth? They didn't

LISTEN to Me–why would you expect them to LISTEN to you?

Forget the arguments of the past. I have forgiven you for those confessed sins. I start you out with a clean slate. Begin again in negotiating. I will give you the the strength to stay away from past offenses. Others past offences are for them to see and to confess. Pray for all. Be at peace. Enjoy your mini vacation ... . Witness in a quiet, gentler way.

10/28/98

My dear Ginny,

When someone sins against you, your first response is a reaction which is not clear to the person who hurt you.

You show your emotion, but not your true feeling. Anger instead of hurt is an example. Next you usually talk about whatever happened to anyone who will LISTEN.

Take all to Me in prayer first. I will show you how to respond. Don't dwell on it. It just continues the pain. In many instances, I will simply ask you to let it go. You have been having many lessons lately. At times you feel pummeled wondering from where the next attack is coming.

When you stay centered on Me, you will be stunned-not wounded.

10/29/98

Dearest one Ginny,

I am love. As you grow closer to Me, you will exhibit more of the qualities. Your patience has already grown. If I gave you all of this love without your seeking and searching and working for it-it would not mean as much.

Keep on desiring to love more. As you LISTEN to Me more carefully, I will show you how to respond. I give you the strength to do the correct thing, but you are still stuck in your old habits, your way of defending yourself both in word and in body language.

A kind and gentle answer or response dampens both your answer and the others response. Come even closer to

Me. Pause-reflect. Slow down especially in the company of those persons to whom you generally over react. Offer your pain of being misunderstood and misinterpreted for the well being of the person who is causing the pain. Use the pain.

11/2/98

Dearest Ginny,

I come to you to give you instruction.

LISTEN closely.

After I rose from the dead, I spent time in the community of Jerusalem with My mother, My apostles and My disciples. Many of them were witnesses of My Resurrection.

After a time of 40 days, I ascended to My Father in heaven where I wait for you to follow Me, to join with Me. At the Last Supper, I left a special gift for you–My Body and My Blood to be consecrated by duly ordained priests. I am present in a truly unique way. I become a part of you as you consume Me. You become a part of Me.

With this privilege comes the awesome responsibility for My children to remain in My grace and thus to help Me to distribute My graces to others. Abide in Me. Live in Me. Dwell in Me. Bring Me to others whom you meet. Keep yourself pure and holy. Cleanse at the Sacrament of Reconciliation, Be purified, loving, merciful and holy.

11/3/98

Dear Ginny,

As I cleansed the temple in Jerusalem to drive out all that had no place in My Father's house, I cleanse your temple. I drive out all sin and all evil and all that is not virtue from your life. I can show you those things which need to be removed, but it is up to you, with your free will, to pick up these vices and sweep them out in confession. If I show you an area in your life which needs forgiveness, and you neglect LISTENING to Me, it is your choice. I am grieved, but I will not force you to change. All change on the outside must begin and end with change on the inside. If the outside appears clean , and the inside is still dirty, the dirt will surface under pressure. A vacuum cleaner bag looks clean on the outside, but, if squeezed when full, the dirt will erupt or ooze through the pores. Be watchful. Repent.

Love, Jesus

11/9/98

Dearest one, Ginny,

All tears will be shed this side of the veil. I wipe away all your tears. Offer them to Me. Grieve and let go. Be present in the moment. Stop going into the past or onward into the future.

I am with you here and now in this chapel on a cold, cloudy autumn day. I am with you whether awake or asleep. I am always aware of the challenges you face. Relax. Let Me guide you. I desire your peace and your health. Allow Me to refresh you. Don't be so hard on yourself. Everything does not have to be in perfect order for Me to love you or for Me to direct you.

LISTEN to Me. LISTEN to your body. LISTEN to your heart.

Pray and do what you will.

I hold you in the palm of My hand. I hug you tight and keep you from all harm.

11/10/98

Dearest Virginia Carol,

You are My servant, not my employee. If you are truly desirous of serving Me, you will LISTEN carefully to My instructions. Nothing is above or beyond the call of duty. You are indentured to Me. You have chosen Me because I have chosen you.

Behave as My servant. Do nothing amiss to bring embarrassment on Me. All who see you should see Me. This is one of the best ways for others to find Me. Those who have seen changes in you are more apt to see Me as they knew what you were once like.

I am your only Master. You may need to obey other legitimate authority-all authority comes from Me. Be of service and I will be served.

12/10/98

Sometimes I come and put My arm around you to offer you comfort. Other times I am off to the side looking lovingly upon you while you decide whether or not to follow My will.

I have allowed you freedom of choice. When you are unavailable to feel My touch, there is more need for you to LISTEN in your heart and to do the correct thing. Sometimes it is right for you to come alongside a friend with comfort in the form of a a hug or a caress to comfort them. Sometimes it is necessary for them for you to remain at a discreet distance so that they can feel their feelings alone and make a decision while you pray for them … . Other times it is best for you to be totally out of the way in prayer.

12/12/98

As you enter into My rest and I come to you, I invite you to more of a relationship with My pain and My suffering as well as with My joy. You will find Me and you will find more of yourself.

Come-come closer.

Do not be afraid. I am always with you.

Hold My hand. Talk with Me. LISTEN to Me. Listen with your heart. Nothing is coincidence. You first allowed Me to bless you here in this chapel with the rest of My Holy Spirit. You invited Me those years ago to take control of you life. Leave this control with Me. Walk in My light and there will be no shadows, no foreboding. LISTEN. Pray. Reflect. Come into Me with all your self. I will give you Myself.

12/16/98

You can trust Me. I keep My word. I am always with you. I care deeply about and for you. I hear and I answer your prayers. Sometimes the answer is on or not now.

Can you be trusted? Are you willing to LISTEN and keep what you have heard in the confines of your heart?

Are you available when others need you? Are you willing to put yourself aside and concentrate on them? Are you willing to let your yes be yes and your no be no?

Learn from your trust in Me what it is that

others need as trust in you.

Go in peace and love everyone.

12/21/98

Inspire others to a genuine devotion to Me. Show them by your demeanor, your attitude and your joy what I have meant to you.

Allow others the opportunity to question your belief as well as your joy. LISTEN to them as I Listen to you. Confirm your response to them by a prayer asking for inspiration from the Holy Spirit. Allow for holy pauses in your usual rapid fire response. Allow your words to be filled with My Love. Check out how they have been received. Review your day at intervals. Give Me more regular opportunities communicate with you until this becomes more habitual with you.

Be not afraid to proclaim Me and My Word. Guard not yourself or your ego. I will care for these. Always be open to those who appear least in the eyes of the world.

Love genuinely.

12/23/98

Happy Birthday

I have been with you on every step of your journey. At times I was pleased with the direction you took. At other times, I was disappointed. Lately more of your steps are in rhythm with Mine. As partners in a dance keep to the same rhythm and are in sync or harmony and display a beautiful image for all to see, so are a person and I when we are in harmony. All can see the beauty. They stop-look -and LISTEN.

People also look and LISTEN and stop at chaos. Feel the rhythm of My step-sense the hand of My will in your life. Allow Me to lead and together there will be a visible beauty.

Keep Me always at the center in all aspects of your life.

I love you Ginny

1/3/99

Dear Ginny,

As I touch the places in your heart that have never seen My holy light before, you will glow with an even more genuine beauty. There will also be more pain as you will become more aware in a very different way. I will be giving you more gifts.

With these gifts will come more responsibility and more accountability to Me on your part. You will be the steward. I will let you know My will. Become more quiet and find more solitude. LISTEN even more closely to Me at all times. Wonder about Me. Smile for Me. Let Me gladden this part of My world with your help. Share your pain with Me.

1/4/99

Abandon yourself to My will. Allow Me to direct your path. LISTEN intently to Me.

Wait for your instructions and carry them out as I ask you to proceed.

Gladly accept the pain and suffering I allow in your life. Offer it all to Me through My mother, Mary. None of it will be wasted. All will advance the salvation of others for whom you are praying. Forget Me not.

Keep My face always in your memory. Hold My hand and

advance with Me towards glory.

1/5/99

Come quickly when I call. As you LISTEN to Me take the short time to discern that it is I.

Do nothing-take no action-no step forward without calling on Me in prayer for confirmation.

All is not well in Kennebunk or in ... . Much prayer and much discernment is necessary. Follow My lead and My example, but check to be certain it is I. Let yourself adapt to My plan. Be flexible. Be willing. Let go of preconceived notions of how I might operate in your life. Be free from sin and love Me and others. Go in peace and My Love.

1/10/99

Whenever you do My will I am pleased. I know that you have taken the time to stop and LISTEN to Me. Take time to stop and LISTEN to others. Let them do more of the talking. LISTEN and pray. Respond to them in love. Involve yourself with Me. Talk of Me to others when they are willing to LISTEN.

Observe body language.

I want all to be with Me in heaven. Be my instrument in having others return to Me. Fix your heart and your eyes on Me and you will be rewarded in heaven.

Go peacefully.

1/19/99

Touch Me, Reach out and touch Me. See Me in those who are around you. See Me in the shadows of your heart. Search for Me. LISTEN for Me. I am never away from you.

Blend yourself with Me. Let others see Me, not you. Find all your peace and security in Me. Be thankful and filled with praise at all times and in all circumstances. By pass the negative. Look at the shadows and see beauty-not darkness. Look at the pain and see the opportunity for healings. Continue in your zeal for speaking of Me with love.

1/23/99

Until you see Me face to face, you will never be as close to Me as you are right now having received Me in My totality in the Eucharist.

Ask what you want of Me. I desire to give you what you long for the most. Don't be shy. Don't be afraid. If what you ask of Me is not good for your salvation, I will not give it to you.

Desire Me. Want to do My will. LISTEN closely as I speak to you in many and varied ways. Look to Me and My mother for you rpeace, sustenance and love. We are always within your grasp.

1/24/99

Light of My heart

Shine forth brightly

Bring the good news

Before the throngs

LISTEN intently

Share from your heart

Give to My people

Your hidden store

Be ever gentle

Be ever kind

Be pure and spotless

Always be Mine

Share on your journey

Care for the crowd

Sense always My Presence

Give all you have

Strength for the journey

Power untold

Will come with the blessings

My Word has forth told

2/3/99

Whenever you take the time to LISTEN or speak with or offer a kindness to one of My people you have offered to Me. Consider this prayer. Love My people. There is so little love in the world and so much selfishness. People are afraid of giving because they are afraid of losing. Unfortunately they are unaware of the rewards in return for giving. Often they are hurt, but so often the joy they give is rewarded with a smile or a toothless grin or a real thank you. They do not know what they are missing in hoarding.

2/13/99

LISTEN. I whisper in the silence. I call you to go forth from here filled with My peace and aware that I have a plan for your life which calls for you to continually turn your will and your way over to Me.

Don't say that you will never do such

and such. This may be what I next
ask of you.

Be open and available. See Me in
the good times and in the bad.
Allow Me to use you as a piece on a
chess board. Trust that I always love
and care for you and yours. Trust,
Trust, Trust

2/14/99

Comfort those who believe that they
are unlovable. Go the extra mile
with an extra smile. It costs nothing
and gives so much.

Trouble yourself for others. Treat
them as your Daddy taught you.
Don't worry about whether they can
do anything for you.

LISTEN to your heart; be aware of what it speaks to you. Be yourself. Stop trying to be otherwise. Select something you can do without and give it away. Give it as a treat to someone in love. Forget yourself for others in My Love.

2/21/99

Allow yourself to relax more in My Presence. Learn to sit patiently and LISTEN to and in the silence. Forget about your problems and your pain once you have shared them with Me. I am not deaf or hard of hearing. It is not necessary for you to repeat yourself to Me.

Once you and your car are on the

ferry, you leave the problems on the land behind. Leave your problems with Me. I will resolve them for you. Move out of the silence to whatever I will.

3/7/99

Respond to Me. LISTEN closely. Come to Me with all your problems and concerns. Walk with Me as your companion–talk with Me as your friend. Allow Me to be your everything. Allow Me to comfort and console you. Allow Me to draw you closer and closer in an intimate relationship.

Show others by your gentle demeanor of My Love and care for you. Follow

My lead. Come and go as I ask. Fulfill your promises to Me. Speak soon to ... or someone else about a general confession.

Go in peace. LOVE

3/9/99

Reject the evils of this world. Do not reject those who commit evil. Find ways to love and pray for them. Speak to them. Instruct them if they are willing to LISTEN. It is of no value, simply a waste of time which could have been spent in prayer, to attempt to instruct any one who is of closed mind and heart. LISTEN carefully to Me, I will show you to whom to go, when, and where.

Complete the tasks I have already given you. Offer to help ... Work on the forgiveness ... spoke of. Be My love.

4/15/99

Together you and I can bring peace and health and happiness to this world of yours. I speak through you and others who have taken the time to LISTEN to me. Some are not yet at a place where they are able to hear Me in their hearts or where they would believe that it is I who am speaking to them. They may LISTEN to you. They may come to believe that I love them and came to bring them Eternal Life. Show them by your attitude and your love and your peace that it is I who have brought you to this place. Pray and love and LISTEN.

4/24/99

Relax. Rest in My arms. My timing is perfect. You need to be rested so that when I call you are able to do what I ask of you.

LISTEN to Me. LISTEN to My creation. Enjoy the sounds of nature. Enjoy the beauty of flowers and sunsets and spring rain and mud.

Allow yourself the time to ponder and wonder at all that surrounds you. Enjoy the chatter of grand children and the noises of teenagers.

Be joyful that you are in the thick of life surrounded by all you can see, hear, smell and touch. Appreciate. Appropriate My love.

6/9/99

Carefully LISTEN to Me. Hear all that I say. Read My Word and LISTEN to its proclamation. Study, then proclaim.

I am with you as you travel throughout your day. I advise and I search you and I allow you to be My emissary. It is important that you LISTEN and are aware of all that is necessary in speaking to someone of Me.

In some instances, it is best for you to

be silent. At other times, I invite you to share the full gospel. Discern carefully what I am asking of you. Move more slowly. Haste creates waste.

6/15/99

Look deeply at Me. Stop turning away. Of what are you afraid? Know that I have already searched you and I know you.

Gaze steadily at Me. I will show you all of yourself. I will allow you to penetrate to the depths of your soul one step at a time. I alone know who you truly are today and who you will become as you allow for more purification. As you already know, this will be painful–but I am with you. Continue to come and worship and adore Me. LISTEN as I speak intimately with you.

6/20/99

Quiet yourself. LISTEN to the sounds of nature. Feel the softness of the breeze. LISTEN to the rhythm of your own breath. I am in control of all. You need not worry about a thing if you quiet yourself and hear Me in the depth of your being. I call to you and you are too busy to LISTEN. I call to you and your mind is cluttered with useless nonsense.

The world and its happenings are Mine. Pray more for those whom you meet.

6/28/99

In the silence of the night I speak to you. In the silence of your pain you are a willing LISTENER. When you are more prepared to LISTEN and to hear My voice in the clutter and chaos of every day living it is all but impossible to search

out My voice from the myriad of noise, unless you are already tuned into My frequency by prayer and self denial.

LISTEN for Me always and you will be receptive to Me when I call on you. Answer in love and trust.

7/4/99

Appropriate the graces I send to you. LISTEN for My call. Do My will.

Find time to bear with others who are carrying heavy loads. LISTEN to their pain. Speak softly in reply. Refrain from giving advice. Allow yourself to become one with them. Let go of yourself and your perceived problems.

After spending time with Me, look at everything with renewed vision.

Pray. Pray. Pray

7/8/99

My invitation ie open for all to come to Me. I have no favorites. I offer each person the opportunity to get to know Me on a personal level.

Thank you for LISTENING to Me. Be even more open and receptive to Me.

I am sometimes hidden in the surroundings of your life. I offer you peace and contentment and you choose chaos. If I don't inspire you to do something, do long hard thinking about it, your inspiration could be in the opposite direction. PRAY

7/23/99

Transform your way of thinking. Continuously ask for My help in this area of your life.

Sin begins in your mind. When you are able, with My aid, to nip these thoughts before they become more alive, you will have a more serene life.

Find yourself praying and praising more and therefor not allowing these thoughts to take hold. LISTEN to My whisper. It can be heard during these thoughts. Throw them out with prayer.

7/30/99

Take My hand and trust that I will bring you to your heavenly goal.

Hardships are necessary, but I am with you.

Remain level headed. Allow yourself the gift of time to discern My way for you. Pause-reflect-LISTEN for My response.

Let others reach out to Me sometimes through you. Don't let them hold on to you because you might be pulled in the wrong direction. When they hold on to Me, they may seem on a different path, but the destination is the same, Heaven.

7/31/99

I am your best friend. I will teach you more about friendship as you let go of your need to have everyone as a friend. Share your deepest joys with Me. I LISTEN and respond.

I alone have all the answers. LISTEN to Me. Go out to others only after you have spoken to Me and this going out is My will.

Many you thought friends have betrayed you. I will never betray you. You have often betrayed yourself. Keep the number of your words down and LISTEN more.

8/6/99

Quarrel not. Do not waste the precious time you have in giving it away before those who would want you to become farther away from Me.

LISTEN to Me. Hear and heed My call. I summon you to come forward and fight for your spiritual life against any and all foes.

Love as I love. Do not harbor resentment or pity.

Praise and thank Me in all circumstances. As you do this, it will become as second nature to you. Fulfill the destiny I have for you. Be alive to Me.

8/15/99

Continue to follow My lead. If necessary, put aside anything and everything else that you deem to be important.

Allow Me to be your sole source of consolation. Others are not always available or are unwilling to LISTEN.

I am always here and am open to you as you pour out your very heart and soul.

As you LISTEN to Me, I will teach you how to LISTEN to others and how much of yourself to share with them, so that

you do not lose part of yourself. Leave it all with Me.

9/7/99

I call to you from the monstrance. I thank you for your visit. I challenge you to let go of everything that is not of Me. I promise to give you all you need to accomplish this end.

I call out. LISTEN. I speak clearly.

You ignore Me. I desire that you be filled with inner peace. I promise this peace if you do My will..

Go forth from here with a smile in your heart and another on your face. Be kind and merciful.

9/29/99

Kneel before Me and feel the warmth on My embrace. Reach out and touch Me in the reality of one another.

Feel My sadness and My pain in yourself and those around. Sense My joy and My peace and My hope.

LISTEN with your heart and your entire body. Let others know you care and are able to do so because of the care and concern I have for you.

Let down your guard. Relax. Be free from worry and restraint. Go in My peace.

10/11/99

I hear your call. I LISTEN. I invite you to wait in patience for Me to prepare the fullness on My love for you. A gift readily available is not as great as one which is given with much preparation. It is worth the wait.

I am preparing you for the greatest gift-eternal life with Me. You will enter into this eternity alone. Learn to seek Me and find Me in your alone ness. I give you My life and My Love. Wait for all the other gifts I will shower on you unexpectedly.

10/12/99

Revitalize your prayer life. See Me before you always extending a hand for you to grasp and to follow. Look more closely into My eyes. See the love I have for all as well as the pain I feel for sin in the world.

Love and pray. Love and pray. Bring My Love everywhere you go. LISTEN to the pain. Love and pray as you LISTEN. Find Me and bring Me with you always.

10/19/99

I fill you with tenderness and strength. These are not contradictions. Without strength your tenderness can be lukewarm and without tenderness your strength is overwhelming.

I am strength under control. Who is more powerful than I? Who is more tender or gentle or merciful than I?

LISTEN to Me. Do My will. Let Me guide you in and out and through and around all the barriers you and others put in your way. Hold on tightly love.

10/20/99

Forgive them. Forgive all who have given you incorrect advice. Forgive those who have hurt you emotionally by ignoring you or your loved ones. Forgive those who have been jealous of you or envious of your possessions. Pray for all of them. LISTEN kindly to them and come to Me for discernment. I allow you to be challenged so that by these challenges you might be purified in body, mind and spirit.

11/6/99

Whenever you want, and wherever you are, you are free to climb into My lap and I will comfort you and give you solace. You do not have to worry that you are monopolizing Me. I have all the time of eternity just for you. I am available to LISTEN whenever you call. You can never abuse My time when you come to Me in love. Stay as long as it takes- forever would not be too long. I long to hold you and give you comfort and solace. Welcome My warm embrace and relax-let yourself abide in Me always

11/7/99

Dearest Ginny,

I invite you to come even closer in a deeper relationship with Me and then I invite you to go out and bring Me to others.

You cannot go if you have not come. You must continue to refresh yourself at the river of My Love. You must nourish yourself with My Word, and you must LISTEN to Me in the quiet stillness of your heart. You cannot give what you do not have. LISTEN and heed. Come and go. Be balanced with Me as center.

12/4/99

Your relationship to Me is not a matter of feelings but of truth.

I am the Way, the Truth and the Life. Follow Me.

I founded a church when I called Peter to be My rock. I have nourished My Church and My truth. I have never once forsaken the Israelites whom I had called.

LISTEN to Me as I speak through My Word and through the authority in My Church. I am love always.

12/7/99

Continue to honor and OBEY and live in Me. Call on Me at ant time of the day or night and I will answer you. LISTEN to your heart. I speak to you in its inner recesses. I call softly in an almost inaudible whisper. You must be focused on Me and tuned in to Me in order to hear.

I speak to you also through My Word and My people. LISTEN and discern.

Be aware of My Presence as I am here with My mother to comfort and console you.

12/8/99

I have heard your cry. I have heard it from the beginning even before you spoke it aloud, even before you were able to put your pain into words. I have been here comforting you and teaching and refining and purifying you.

Sometimes you pushed even shoved Me away. You have not always been receptive to My help. Continue to call-even holler and I will LISTEN, LISTEN to Me in the depths of your heart and I will heal you pain even when the problem continues.

12/21/99

I inspire you to do My will. LISTEN to Me. LISTEN as I speak to the deepest recesses of your heart and soul. LISTEN as I whisper words of love and of longing to you. LISTEN as I direct you to uphold My truth so that it I now watered down. Do this with dignity and love. Show others that love consists in doing My will and following My commands. Be fruitful. Multiply My words as you speak them to others.

12/30/99

Spontaneity, joy, laughter, fun, frolic are part of My plan for you. It is never necessary nor even wise for you to go about with a glum look on your face.

Hardship and trials come and they go. I come and I stay. LISTEN. LISTEN closely as I call you to follow Me into Eternity. Eternity begins here and now and with each step forward brings you closer to Me. Your eyes become more open as do your ears as you follow Me more closely.

1/4/00

When Adam and Eve sinned by eating of the knowledge of good and evil, they lost supernatural touch with Me. They let go of their trust in Me. They LISTENED to themselves and the serpent because they thought they knew better.

In this eating they then had a natural understanding of good and evil–the natural law. I never left them unaided as I never have left you unaided.

When you choose to do My will and are in the state of grace, I offer you supernatural gifts. You are free to use or to reject them. The more you use them, the brighter they become in you as patina on a regularly used silverware shines. It is not dull.

1/16/00

Rejoice. I am with you. I love you.

I desire to give you your heart's desire. I desire to shower you with My Divine grace. Be open and receptive.

LISTEN as I speak in the quiet recesses of your mind and heart. Do not quell My Spirit. Advance when I invite you to move. Quiet the longings of your heart. Allow Me alone to be the one you long for. I alone can fill your needs. Others come in and out of your life. No one other than I has been with you since the beginning and will be with you in the end.

Detachment is the letting go of the intense need you have for human comfort and consolation. Rely on Me.

I am all in all. Relax. Be at peace.

1/19/00.

Reclaim all that I have set aside for you. You have overlooked some of the gifts I have given to you. You have left them unopened in their lovely wrappings because you were afraid of what might be inside. You have learned by LISTENING to Me that sometimes I have sent you persecution and pain.

As you travel along the road with Me as on the road to Emmaus, I share with you. Often you are unaware that it is I.

Open the package I have sent and those I will send. I know more than anyone what it is that you really need for your eternal journey. Nothing I send will ever need to be returned until you have satisfied the reason for My sending it. Share My gifts with others who are open and unafraid.

2/3/00

Talk with Me about whatever it is bothering you. Let Me hear you speak your pain and your frustration so that you can receive an answer from Me.

Allow yourself to absorb the comfort I am here to offer to you.

Spend more time in silence before Me.

Allow yourself to absorb the comfort I am here to offer to you.

LISTEN attentively to My voice in the silence. Allow Me to inspire you.

Shallow people have shallow thoughts and ideas. Pray for them. Pray for all I put in your path.

Confine yourself to speaking only to a few trusted, sincere friends and you will not open yourself and your old wounds to contamination.

Continue to pray for your family and friends. I do love you.

2/5/00

Devote yourself to Me and My message of truth. I am Truth. I desire all to be in Heaven with Me for all eternity.

LISTEN as I speak to you. Act if this action is prudent. Pray otherwise. I am known to offer change to hearts of those for whom My committed ones pray.

Return more frequently to My arms and those of My blessed mother. We want to enfold you, offer you peace and comfort and encourage you in your pilgrimage.

Look closely at Me in My Blessed Sacrament. I am exposed and vulnerable. You are here present in the church to protect Me as I do not move physically from here. Your protect Me. I protect you. Long for Me at all times. Call on Me when you start to trip. I will protect you from falling.

2/7/00

Quiet yourself. Quit running. Do those things I ask of you and those things to tranquility and order into your surroundings.

Spend less time on the telephone and more time talking and LISTENING to Me.

When you are offended let it go in My direction. As I have expressed before- feel the pain and move on. Allow Me to apply My healing and soothing salve, balm of love, to those wounds which keep being reopened. Soon they will be healed and there will be no more pain in those areas.

Dwell in Me. Rest in Me. Allow Me to comfort and console you. I have not asked you to solve all the problems your find yourself in. When you react you become wound up on problem and solution like a knotted string. Stay loose. LISTEN. Respond. Pray. Love.

3/6/00

I, Almighty God, bend down and LISTEN to your prayer. Some pain is so great that it is impossible to form words–I bend down and LISTEN.

Some pain is unknown but only felt. It cannot be formed into words–there are none. I bend down and LISTEN. Some pain touches nerve endings in such a way that the prayer is a shriek or a scream. Some may think that I would cover My ears and retreat. I bend down and LISTEN.

In the postureof bending, I am better able to put My arm around and to comfort and console. I provide shelter and warmth in this posture.

LISTEN to others. Bend down to them. Let go of your fear of rejection. Be available. Comfort–don't cover your ears. Let the other release all his pain to Me through you; the, be Me to comfoprt and console. Bend down and LISTEN. You will hear Me speak to you.

3/10/00

Thank you for coming to visit. Thank you for caring for My friends this morning. Thank you for your willingness to take better care of yourself. You will need to be in good health to perform the task to which I am calling and for which I am preparing you.

LISTEN to My voice. LISTEN to your heart. Disregard

discord and disharmony. Pray to break the hold of any and every negative thought.

Smile in the midst of all I send or allow to be sent to you. As you have become stronger in your desire to do My will. I have sent you more to do. Leave your worries with Me. If I ask you to do something, I will give you the where with all to accomplish it. Just look at Mother Angelica and Mother Theresa.

3/19/00

Look forward with hope and joy to the times you spend alone with Me. Treasure them.

You will not always be able to come to Me on a daily basis. You will want to recall these special quiet times here when we conversed. When this time comes I will come to you and visit wherever you are. Thank you for spending this time with Me. Thank you for becoming more and more open and receptive to a more silent way of life. There is much further to go, but you have already taken many steps in the right direction.

Follow wherever I lead you. Let go of all your own anger and resentment and do only what I ask of you. You have frequently mistaken your own idea for mine and you will continue in this manner until you have made the whole of your life a prayer.

I call. You LISTEN, sometimes. LISTEN more closely. Confirm My call with your caller ID. Ask me for confirmation. I will respond.

LISTEN LISTEN

4/7/00

When I speak to you, LISTEN. My words are those of love and peace and strength for your journey towards Me.

I offer you My Word and My sacraments. I offer you My hand to hold. I offer you the totality of the graces available to you simply for the asking. I offer you the opportunity to suffer and to die to self for Me and for your neighbor.

Take My hand. I will guide you. I am the Way. I show it to you. Take My Word and make it yours. Take My sacraments and be nourished for your journey.

LISTEN intently. Leave the talking to Me. Let go of your need to talk of your problems. Grow and glow with and for Me.

4/13/00

Have confidence in Me and in My Love for you and for all.

As you love your children by setting boundaries for their behavior, I set boundaries for My children.

Law is not to restrict, but to offer freedom from harm. A one way street sign alerts the driver to go only left or right. Someone has determined that this is best for order, not chaos.

LISTEN to My one way signs. Be on the alert for those things I ask you to refrain from for your betterment and the betterment of others.

Keep in mind that I created you. I do not want to curtail your freedom. I want to protect you from harm both physical and spiritual.

4/17/00

Silence and peace are the fruits of LISTENING and love.

The silence and the peace are interior gifts. I give them to you as you come closer to Me. You have a long way to go. You have only uncovered one of the many veils or layers that keeps you from seeing Me face to face.

The last veil will be lifted on the other side of eternity. There is still a long way to go. Just imagine the peace I have to offer to you.

4/20/00

Insult and injury came My way. Can you expect to avoid them if you say you want to be My follower?

I gave My beard to be plucked. This means that someone intruded very closely into My space. I allowed this to occur. I was to die for your sins.

Whenever someone encroaches too closely into your space, ask Me what you should be doing. Sometimes you are to accept this for the benefit of both your souls. The other may be testing you in order simply to provoke you to react. If you pause and LISTEN to Me, I may invite you to relax and rsepond in a kind and gentle way. You may need to do this to help that soul come to a closer relationship with Me. LISTEN to Me. Respond in love united with prayer. I am the Way, the Truth, and the Life.

5/3/00

Allow Me to show you My way. Allow

Me to comfort and console you.
Allow Me to leave you My plan for your salvation and sanctification.
Allow Me to be your all in all.

Witness My Love for you to others.
Witness My deep concern and care for you.

LISTEN carefully for My call.
Discern My voice.

I know the pain you experience for those who are not following Me closely. I hear your cry of pain. I LISTEN.

Continue to call out to Me. I will answer. It will not be easy, but it will be necessary.

5/13/00

Release yourself. Let go of all that I do not send to you. Become untangled and unglued from persons, places and things that I have not sent you.

How can you do My work and My will when you are burdened with other people's business.

Love others, but do not attach yourself to them. Leave them and you unsullied and unencumbered.

Lay down your life and your burdens for Me. Give Me the totality of your attention. LISTEN, Don't always speak.

See and hear the boundaries others have set. Be careful of your limits.

Limit yourself to My will.

5/14/00

Believe that I desire to fill you with the warmth of My tender love. I want to set you so on fire with My love that you will be a beacon of love and peace to others.

Be not afraid. I love you. I am with you.

Your struggles will increase, but so will your peace and serenity. You have been LISTENING to Me. I will be using you more and more for My work. You must persevere in the patience you have been learning.

If you are impatient, rude or rash,

others will not see Me and the mission will be aborted.

5/30/00

Alleluia

I am risen. I am here with you. I desire to have you LISTEN closely to what I have to say.

All were created by Me. All have the possibility of redemption if they come and follow Me.

Allow Me access to the deepest parts of yourself. Allow Me to defrost those area which have become frozen by years of denial. Allow Me to thaw you out.

LISTEN and then process with My

help. I long for you to understand MY ways. I long for you to filter the truth from all the impure particles you have been given. I have gifted you with a strong, vibrant faith in Me. Use your faith, your knowledge, and your love of Me to open My truth to yourself and to others whom I send to you. Go in peace. I will continue speaking to you.

6/1/00

Nervous energy is not really energy at all,.it is impulsiveness. Power under control is the energy which can best used for Me as one does My will.

Be willing more and more to quiet yourself and see Me. See Me beckoning you to come and visit with Me. Let Me speak to you in your heart as you LISTEN to it pulsate. I do not require haste. Your life is not an emergency. You do not need to make haste like a steam engine spewing your steam for all to see. When you glide along, you will have much smoother sailing; waste no energy, hurt no one on your way, and arrive at the time I have appointed.

I ascended into heaven in My full glory. I sent My Holy Spirit to be with you to guide and to comfort you. I allow you your free will. I invite you even closer in your bond with Me. I call you by name. I summon you to follow My will. I offer you all the energy needed for the tasks I appoint. Don't bolt. Don't hesitate. Follow Me.

6/6/00

Satan has a plan to kill all of My disciples. It is not necessary that he kill body but that he kill the spirit. I protect any and all who call on Me. I give all the defenses to defeat Satan and his devils. I equip you with all the necessary tools. You have the power of My name and of My blood to defeat him in any and all battles. I am the victor. I have already conquered Satan.

In LISTENING to My voice, you will

know when you are in a battle. The struggle is real. It is a struggle of good and evil. Each struggle is different. Each struggle must be won. Are you ready for the battle? I give you My grace and My peace as protection.

7/29/00

May My warmth envelop and embrace you.

May you walk sprightly and upright by My side.

May you call on Me in all your endeavors.

May you LISTEN to Me in the silence and for Me in the midst of all the clamor.

May your love for all exceed your greatest expectations.

May you flow in Me as in a river.

May you abide in My Love and find rest in the midst of your journey.

May you forgive all who have offended you.

May you find shelter from the storms of life and rejoice in the beauty of the day.

May your desire to spend eternity with Me never waver.

May you know and feel My intense desire for you.

10/22/00

You are always rushing in and out

these days and not taking time to LISTEN to me in the deepest part of your heart.

I have been calling you to go forth and help your neighbor, but I have been trying to get your attention to LISTEN to Me. I have not stopped speaking to you in the silence of your heart.

I have much more direction to give you. I am not finished dialoguing with you.

Slow down. Spend time alone discerning My will for you. Let Me lead you deeper within your own being to an ever deeper, calmer, more satisfying relationship with Me.

Do you love Me?

Do you want to do My will?

Quiet yourself. LISTEN and believe that I speak to you in love. Go in peace.

10/28/00

Relax. I am in control. I love you and honor you as My child.

Respect all who come into your life. Do My will, not yours. Let go of all criticism. Fill your life with days of revelation and praise of My glory.

Stop resisting Me. Be open and vulnerable when I call.

See everyone as your brother or sister in Christ.

It is not sinful to be rich or belong to clubs. Stop minding other people's business and get on with your own life.

Learn more of Me from My Word.
Learn more of My church.

Love Me in the way I ask of you.
Learn to follow My directions.

Slow down. LISTEN more. Talk less.
Let others come to know and love you more slowly.

Be still and know that I am God-you are not. Calm down. Enjoy.

11/4/00

Come dine with Me at the foot of the cross.

Receive Me into your soul as well as your body. Allow Me to transform you into an image of Myself. Allow Me to melt you and mold you as I treasure and love and purify you.

Come to Me with all your successes and your failure. Come sit by Me and speak lovingly to Me of your heart aches and your joys.

Be silent with Me. Allow Me to do the talking. Allow Me to instruct you in My ways. Allow Me more freedom and the flexibility to show you more deeply of My ways.

Stand back. LISTEN. Allow Me to speak through you and I will give you My peace which surpasses all your understanding. AMEN

11/5/00

Release all you have and all you are into My tender, gentle, wounded hands. There is no need for you to carry any of it. All I have is yours and all you have is Mine. Give it to Me. I will tenderly and gently take all your joys and sorrows and burdens. What is a Friend for?

Stop trying to control everything. Stop putting yourself in places where you are torturing yourself for a reason.

I call you out of the fire and into the fire of My Divine Love. LISTEN and learn. I am your only Way.

11/18/00

LISTEN to your own tears of grief for the loss of your marriage. Like your lost earring, there is not one thing you can do about it. You can save the other earring in a safe place in the event the lost one turns up, but you should not keep it in a special place of honor so that you will always be reminded of the loss. You returned to the area when you lost your earring and searched high and low. It is of no use for you to return there again today. It would only cause you to think you were stupid to have ever lost it in the first place. It is gone. You did not and should not go out and replace it with a replica. You moved on and have found other earrings to wear.

Move on. Find other topics and areas of interest. Let the dead bury the dead. Hold My hand and allow Me to show you all My treasures which you have been missing while focusing on your lost marriage.

AMEN ALLELUIA

1/9/01

I hear your voice. I hear you calling Me. I LISTEN. I answer. None of your cries or sighs goes unheard or unanswered.

When My answer is yes, you generally hear it loud and clear. Sometimes it is softer and you only see the answer at a later time.

When My answer is wait or maybe or no, you may need to stoop and LISTEN more closely.

Whatever My answer, it is always for the greater benefit of your soul. The soul for whom you requested something may have refused it. Always acknowledge, praise and thank Me.

1/19/01

Look at Me and feel My pain for society. LISTEN to Me. I ask your help in alleviating some of this pain.

My pain was and is caused by sinful man. Be a bearer of My truth. Be stalwart. Keep on keeping on in the midst of depravity.

Someone is LISTENING and will come closer to Me because of what you have said or done whilst carrying out My Will.

You are not alone. I am with you. Other disciples are beside you either physically or spiritually through prayer. Persevere. I trust your promises to Me.

2/2/01

I allow you the freedom to fail. I offer you the grace to succeed in those endeavors to which I call you.

Failure in man's eyes may be success in Mine. All things happen for the good.

I will succeed in My plan with or without your help. I will for you to become perfected. You are free to choose good or evil in each and every situation.

Since you have offered Me your will, I offer you the guidance. LISTEN closely to Me and you will choose the good. I love you.

3/29/01

What is a friend?

A friend is someone who lets you be yourself and doesn't try to change you.

A friend is one who loves you for who you are, and not for what you can do for him or her.

A friend is one who will correct you if this is necessary.

A friend will share your joy and your pain; one who will LISTEN and respond.

A friend is the person who is present to you in the thick and thin.

A friend wills the best for you always.

I am the only one who is always there for you. Share all with Me. Friends have limitations of time and energy.

6/1/01

Be open and remain open to receive

My everlasting love. LISTEN to Me and LISTEN to others. Hear their pain and then direct them to Me for the answer to their dilemma.

Foster love among others. Use the skills and the gifts I have given you to offer strength and solace.

Allow Me to be the director of all that you do and say. Free yourself of all that is useless and dead like washing off an old layer of skin and then seeing the freshness of the new layer. Depend on Me. Call on Me. Suffer with Me and, most of all, Trust on Me.

SHINE-GLOW

6/2/01

Come into My Presence. Look into My face. My eyes behold you and search you and seek your love.

I sent My Holy Spirit to nourish you and give you strength for the eternal journey. I nourish you with MY Body and Blood, Soul and Divinity in the Eucharist. I call and you LISTEN at times. Other times I call and you offer Me a deaf ear. LISTEN closely. Fall on your knees in adoration. Give My love back to Me and your love for others will increase dramatically.

6/22/01

I desire you to do My will and that of My Father. This will is that you always do what your informed conscience tells you. Search your heart and follow Me. Do whatever We tell you, LISTEN to Us speak and confirm the message with what you already know in your mind and heart to be the truth. Never follow unless you have checked out the directions first with Us. Our directions always lead to eternal life. No detours on this course.

8/4/01

Will you be My follower? Will you LISTEN more closely to My warnings and My words? Will you put yourself aside to serve the others I put in your path? Will you do My will, not your own? Will you follow wherever I lead you? Will you go into the desert dry and without food and water for body or soul? Will you go into tempests ans storms without an umbrella or a raincoat? If you are to follow Me closely you must do this and much, much more. Yours is the choice.

8/7/01

LISTEN when I speak to you. I always offer you the grace to let go and move on. You refuse this grace and also many others I off you throughout the day.

You say that you want My help, but you proceed often on your own like a bull in a china shop.

LISTEN to Me. Stop and reflect on what you are thinking BEFORE going on into an action. Forget yourself and your pain. Focus on Me and you will gain peace in the midst of your pain. You don't want to let go because thinking and talking and acting out around ... has become a crutch for you. You say you want to move on, but you cannot run with Me if you are carrying a crutch. You keep tripping and sliding and falling instead of gliding and flying and soaring with Me. I don't ask you to forget.

I don't ask you to discontinue praying. I do ask you not to use ... to continue in your pain.

Leave your pain here with Me.

Go out from this chapel free from even the smallest thread which binds you to the hurt and keeps you from total healing.

....

Keep moving forward with love. Use all the energy I give you for good. Stop complaining and criticizing. Pray, pray, and then pray more

I am the Savior of the world–not you. Leave Me to My work. Find pleasure in My world and its creatures. Love and you will find peace. Let go of the years of clutter. Make space for new experiences especially that of peace and love and caring.

10/12/01

LISTEN to your heart. This where I speak with you.

I tell you of My love. I move you closer and closer to doing My will whenever you hear Me and act.

Until you do the first thing and do it well, I cannot invite you to do the next. Each time you do My will, I invite you into a deeper walk and dialogue with Me. LISTEN closely. I love you.

11/3/01

My line is never busy. I am available to you at all hours of the day or night to LISTEN to you and respond.

My number is easy to remember, just call out to Me and I will answer.

Stop wasting time and money on long distance calls which can never fully satisfy. Leave your problems with Me. Go, have fun.

12/31/01

Come. Bend. Worship. Pray. Praise. Love. Live. Forgive. Let go. Allow. Persuade. Pursue. Follow. Guide. Protect. Provide. Reassure. Beware. Be calm. Nurture. Touch. Allow. Prevent. Act. Respond. Be alive. Sit still. Fast. Pray. LISTEN. Forgive. Be silent. Share.

Allow Me to be your God. Leave here tonight filled with My peace and My presence. Learn to not only LISTEN to Me , but to hear Me in the depths of your heart and make a firm decision to do as I ask. You will never regret this advice. Just do it! Now!

1/1/02

Speak to Me of your fears and of your failures.

Speak to Me of your love and your life.

Speak to Me of your longings for peace and happiness in your family and with your friends and in the world.

Spend more time this year in LISTENING to Me and others.

Hold on to your opinions unless you are invited to share them.

Leave all your burdens with Me as soon as you begin to notice them. Don't allow them to burden you when I am just a short prayer away and am waiting to protect you from them by carrying them for you. I have already suffered all My pain.

1/4/02

Comfort those who are in pain in the way you would want to be comforted unless I show you otherwise.

Hand your skills on to those who seek you out.

Look at your problem or your plan before you move forward with it.

Allow yourself to be led by Me.

Fall on your knees in adoration of Me whenever I ask.

Put your dreams on hold and follow My call. Your own dreams and wishes for yourself pale in comparison to what I have in store for you.

Do not be afraid. I am with you. I call. You need only to respond.

Leave your angst and anxieties and your pains will follow. Let it all go. LISTEN and obey.

1/9/02

LISTEN with your heart, not with your head. Hear and heed My Word and act on it in love. Do what I ask, not what you think you ought to do.

Be obedient and you will find the peace you run around searching for. This peace has always been within your grasp. It is the feeling you enjoy when seeing a pink sun rise or sun set or observing a rainbow after a storm. There is nothing you can do to alter My sky. I am the One in charge. You only need appreciate what I send.

You enjoy snow on a cloudy day-it does not depress you as it may others-it gives you a feeling of warmth and comfort. Enjoy all these moments, but first find comfort in all I send your way. OBEY Me and you will find the peace which often alludes you. You will be able to keep this peace if you stay present to Me.

2/26/02

LISTEN as I speak to you. Not to harm you do I allow problems to be yours. I am in the process of purifying you. I want to remove all the dross from you. In order to do this you must be more still. I desire to teach you more of MY ways. I want you to grow in faith, hope and love. When you are self satisfied, your reliance is not on Me. I want you to rely totally on Me.

LISTEN as I speak to your heart and soul. Speak to others of My love for them. Help them to be willing to LISTEN to Me also.

Forgive the transgressions of others against you. Free them to search for Me. They will have their own trials. Pray for them to persevere. I love all My children as you love yours, only more.

3/8/02

Continue to love Me. Continue to offer prayers and sacrifice for My priests. Continue to fulfill and follow the path I have laid out for you.

LISTEN to the sound of My call. Act

on it. Love others as you love Me. Ask them to witness of their lives and share yours. I may send you to people and places that may seem strange to you at first. I have My reasons. Cover yourself with My blood through prayer and you will survive these errands.

I do not ask you to do for others what they are capable of doing for themselves. I do ask you to put yourself out on a limb for Me. I hold up the limb and I hold you in the palm of My hand.

3/28/02

Life in Me is about trust in Me. When you trust in Me you are free to relax, rest, abide, flow, and let go. When you are rigid, firm, taut and inflexible you get hurt.

Trust in Me means giving Me the right to tell you My way.

You do not need to trust in others to abide in Me. Sometimes in your trusting Me you will be hurt by the other. I have a lesson to teach you and the other. When you are resting in Me the hurt will not decimate you. It will lay you low for a time. Use this time to seek Me more closely and LISTEN to the message I have for you.

Trust in Me. Do My will. Allow Me to continue to soften and mold you. Stop being so inflexible. You can hurt yourself when you fall on the ice, but the danger is much reduced if you fall into the water at the same place during the summer. You will get wet and you may be refreshed. Let yourself go and you will grow in Me and My love.

4/23/02

I see clearly. You see dimly. You see only shadows while I see the entire picture. Let Me unfold more of the picture for you to see as My cross is uncovered little by little on Good Friday.

My picture might appear as a quilt with each of My servants responsible for one or more squares. Each time you LISTEN to Me and choose My will and My way, you sew another stitch so to speak. I give you the threads, but you do not know the color or texture. Suffering and pain offered in love sew the most brilliant of colors. Be part of My brilliance. LISTEN to Me and keep close to Me.

9/3/02

LISTEN while I speak. I have a plan for you and for your life. Every time you complain,, you thwart the plan, you delay it, you cause Me to take more time in its fulfillment.

LISTEN to Me not to yourself and what you perceive as your latest problem. These thoughts and these obsessions are not of Me. They are a plan on the part of the evil one to get you out of focus- to blur your vision- to side track you. Stay on track- the one that leads to an eternity with Me. Balance as you would on the track of My will and My plan. Each time you become unbalanced, you derail and time is wasted as I assist you back on track. I love you. Go in peace and serve others.

10/4/02

In the depths of your heart it is dark and quiet, but also alive and full of life in Me. I always speak to you in these depths, but you are often not aware due to the busyness with which you surround yourself.

Go to this quiet place often. Feel the beating of your natural heart and My life which pulses through you. Never take My love and My life in you for granted. Live a life of prayer and service. Serve Me in others. I place them in your path–notice them. Feel for them, but do not try to eradicated their pain–simply LISTEN to their pain and their joy.

Come into silence more when you are in the presence of others. They will be rewarded.

10/5/02

My will for you is just that–My will for you alone. You are as is everyone,

one of a kind. I have a role for you that no one else will fill. Each of you is a part of My plan for eternity. Each is special. Each has a definite purpose. I do not expose My ultimate plan. I invite you one step, one prayer, one action at a time. If you do not follow My will, I will re invite you. I know in advance when and where you will follow. My plan will not be thwarted.

LISTEN closely. Follow Me. Come. Do My will. Be with Me forever in an eternity which has already begun here on earth. I love you. Love others with My Love.

4/11/03

When I sit or kneel here waiting or hoping for you to speak with Me, I often feel I am wasting time.

In the silence of your heart is an area so large you cannot comprehend it. You will never fathom the heights or depths of this gift I have given you. You can exercise yourself by setting your mind and heart on Me ans reach areas you didn't think were possible. Sometimes I call you into the silence and speak. Sometimes you call Me and I am silent. LISTEN in the silence. Learn to modify your tendencies to always be alert. Slow down on the inside as well as on the outside.

Time spent with Me is never wasted or wrong. You are on a journey and I am your Guide. Sometimes we go to look at beautiful flowers and meadows and mountains and lakes, and at other times, we go through arid, dry, lonely deserts. I am with you on every journey. Follow where I lead and every day will be an adventure in silence, in dryness and in fruitfulness. Join Me.

4/17/03

Dear Lord Jesus,

Once again I decide to offer you my will and to do Yours. Take My heart and fill it with love for you. Thank you for coming to me in Holy Communion.

All of your life silence has been difficult for you, but you have persevered. Ever since you were small, you have tried to offer Me three hours on Good Friday. I commend you. This comes easily for others.

I have asked you to be silent more frequently. You have heard Me , but you have not complied. LISTEN to Me when I speak. I speak only to you in the silence of your heart. When you are silent, you will see that it becomes easier for you to do My will. I don't ask of you anything that you are incapable of doing.

Focus more of your supernatural life on reclaiming those parts of yourself that have been damaged over the years. I will show you when and how.

I ask you regularly to mind your own business in many situations. Obey Me in this.

Peace comes surely and swiftly when you follow My direction

5/3/03

Dear Lord,

What are the secret monsters or fears that you are asking me to be more aware of?

5/21/03

My child,

You are your own biggest monster. You are so sure of yourself that you forget that I am the Lord of your life.

Even when you think you have slowed down, you are still running at a pace that wears you out. You are afraid that you won't remember what you are to do or say next. You continue to forget to slow down or stop to LISTEN to Me. You think if you don't act in a frantic way that the opportunity at hand will pass. If it does, and you have stopped to LISTEN to Me, you will have more opportunities.

I am God. You are not. You are

Ginny and you are fearfully and wonderfully made by Me. Don't worry or even wonder what others think of you, if you are in My will. It is none of their concern what you do with your time. I am the Master of your time when you turn yourself over to Me.

Relax. Rest. Revive. LISTEN and I do speak to you.

4/29/04

Both of my ears are totally blocked with wax.

LISTEN.

I speak from within.

I speak to your heart, not to your ears.

I unfold My mysteries in silence.

The hub bub of background noises confuse all who want to hear Me,

LISTEN in the silence.

Listen to your heart as it speaks to you.

Silence the chaos and confusion.

Concentrate on Me alone.

Drown out the world's mighty drove.

Glimpses of Me are found everywhere.

All of Me is contained in your soul.

Quiet all the challenges of the world.

Become aware of My Presence.

Learn to return to the place of

silence.

Submit to Me and you will find peace.

Come home to your heart.

Rest in and with Me.

Love and love will return.

Love not with your body but with your heart.

Feel your heart reaching in for Me and out to others in compassion, mercy, gentleness and peace.

Be calm, serene, loving and peace filled.

2/9/05

Ash Wednesday

LISTEN closely as I speak to you. Bend your ears and open your heart to all that I have to offer to you.

Become little in your own eyes. Desist from defending yourself in any situation. Allow the other to talk until he or she has exhausted his or her supply of words and the be silent until I invite or encourage you to speak. This will be very difficult for you at first, but I will shower My graces on you like mist. Look for them and you will sense them in the quiet atmosphere of your repentant and open heart.

As you LISTEN more and accept more of My graces, your heart will soften and begin to melt and open more and more as you become vulnerable to Me. I will you protect from any hurts harming you. You will be hurt, but remember, so was I, and I am holding your hurts for you. Love extraordinarily.

2/14/05

Dearest Lord Jesus,

Help me to know how to discern Your voice when there are noises all around.

My dear Ginny,

My voice is soft and clear and gentle. I do not scream to be heard, but I speak in a whisper. When you have LISTENING ears of faith and are truly desirous of doing My Will, you must slow down and LISTEN. I will speak.

You asked to be used by Me. You offered to suffer for your family. Realize that you are part of My family and all I have is yours. I ask you to realize that your suffering does have value and to stop complaining and move on in trust to do what you promised to Me. I will always do what I have promised. Take one step at a time. LISTEN more in the silence.

2/15/05

Dear Lord Jesus,

Why am I crying?

My dear Ginny,

You are crying because you can relate to Paul. He is being imprisoned and persecuted for knowing and for sharing the Truth about Me and about My ways.

Paul has at this time a need to defend himself before those in Jerusalem, some of whom had know him or of him for years. Generally he did not offer defense , and on many occasions, he walked away when he was dismissed by the crowds.

Paul had always longed to do My will. Even when he was persecuting the Christians, he thought he was doing My will. When he fell of his horse and had a face to face encounter with Me, he knew he had been wrong and repented. He never stopped loving Me and doing My Will even unto his death.

LISTEN. I will guide you

3/5/05

Dearest Jesus,

What is mercy?

Mercy is the sum total and each individual gift that I give to you on My path and to show you My way. Mercy comes in oh so many different packages. Sometimes it is easy to see but other times it is so well wrapped that unless you take the time to remove the wrappings you will not see the fullness of the gift. I am mercy and love and forgiveness and your true way.

Each time you receive or give of Me, you are involved in some act of mercy. There is no fullness that I can give you at this time to cover all the mercy I give even to you. Keep alert and LISTEN and you will be able to delve deeper into this wonderful mystery.

Mercy is My love,
Mercy is My life.

Mercy gives you peace.

Mercy shows you the way.

Mercy removes sin.

Mercy unlocks mysteries.

Mercy is forever and free.

Give mercy ,and like a boomerang. It will return to you. This boomerang may go a long way and a long time, but it will return to you disguised as another gift from Me. Pain is mercy in disguise.

4/22/05

My dear one,

You are My child, but you often run to others instead of coming to Me. I want to show you that I am here for you always and that I will not meet your needs. You are usually surrounded by luxury which makes it easier for you to think you can go it alone. This weekend many things will not go the way you would have designed. Let it go. Go with the flow. Don't complain. See how others live when they are compacted together and must survive. Serve the others and don't count the cost.

LISTEN. Refrain from your usual useless chatter. Let others have the first and the last word.

Come closer to Me and allow Me to minister to you through ... and others who may appear clumsy to you.

You will return home a more fulfilled and joy filled woman of

4/23/05

Father, why did you bring me here?

I invited you to taste of the goodness of My love. I invited you to come even closer to Me in both Word and Sacrament. I long to get you to really know who I am. I want you to rediscover the gifts I have given you.

Sit back and LISTEN.

LISTEN to My people. Be open and learn from them.

Realize that you are not alone. There are others who want to know Me as you do. There are others who want to know each other in Me.

You are not alone.

Others do believe as you do.

4/24/05

My little one,

Each time you feel another's pain and look into his or her face with compassion, you are offering to help Me carry My cross.

Sometimes you offer a hand to get up, sometimes you chat over a cup of coffee, sometimes you share your own past pain so you become real, sometimes you LISTEN, sometimes you pray and sometimes you even avoid because you put yourself first for selfish reasons.

You have asked to be part of My work and I have taken you at your word. Continue to reach out to others even when you are tormented and teased by the standers by. Whenever you reach out in love, you have tried to do My will. You will sometimes be out of My will. Don't discontinue. Try to LISTEN more.

You are loved. You are a treasure. You feel with and for Me. I love you and will work with you for you to conform more closely to My will more regularly.

7/12/05

LISTEN and I will speak. Take each moment as it comes and cherish it. It will never return again.

2/13/06

Dear Lord Jesus,

We were canceled on a flight home yesterday due to a blizzard in New England. Was there a specific reason you invited me to stay here today?

I love You, Ginny

My dearest Ginny,

You have begun to LISTEN. You heard Me in the delay of your flight. It is not necessary for you to know and understand at this time.

You have come to visit Me at My invitation. This is an added day of rest for you. It takes time for you to adjust to change and I have given you time.

The priest you have now seen three

times needs your prayer at this time. He is holy and wants to continue that way, but is being pushed by others. Pray for him now.

Be gentle with .... Relax around them.

Invite Me into your heart

Give Me the best of your life

Refrain from vanity and pride

Summon others to Me

Share your gift

Forget your pain

Love without thought of pain

Forgive and love again

3/4/06

I invited You came

I called You answered

I summoned You followed

I spoke You LISTENED

I am hurt You feel the pain

I am Love You must love

I offer you all that I Am and all that I have and you are reluctant to see this. Your life can be filled with Me as you desire. Empty out all the hard feelings, bitterness, resentment, and criticism and be filled with My love and joy and peace to be radiated to others. As you know, the heat can be coming up to the radiator, but if it is not turned on, no heat comes into the room. Turn the valve of your heart all the way on and radiate the warmth of My love.

Release all the air from the pipes so that just warmth exudes from you. Do this for Lent and expect it to become a virtuous habit.

3/12/06

Behold, I see your face

Behold, I know of your love

Come, offer Me your pain

Make your presence felt to Me

Reach out with your heart and touch Me

Reach out with your mind and love me

Reach out with your will and respond

Come as a child–leave fulfilled

Come as you are but humbled

Search for Me always

Seek Me with your all

Forgive those who disturb you

Forgive and let Me help you forget

Search don't research

LISTEN to My voice in the silence

3/30/06

You are concerned about many things. All are My concern. Do not hesitate in your love. It may not be returned as you would wish, but you will have done your part. I will be with you as will My mother. I alone can change hearts. You are in My heart and so are .... As you were told a year ago, do the next right thing. Hold firmly to My hand and I will lead you in truth and victory. One never loses when one loves even if one is hurt.

Pray for your visit. LISTEN for Me before you speak. Hold your tongue. Expect nothing. You will gain everything.

Do not be afraid, I am with you.

Let go of your fears. Smile. Be gentle. Be open and forgiving. I will sustain you.

4/26/06

I shower My Mercy on you

I give you My tender love

I wash you in My blood

I hover over you

Increase your grace by following My lead instead of running ahead of Me. My Mercy flows over you when you take up the rear. You miss it when you rush head strong before Me.

Be fruitful and multiply the gifts I have given you. You will not see this but it will occur. Share your blessings with others who are willing to LISTEN. Share your prayers with all.

Give and it will be given to you. I am the giver.

Because of apostles like you and others, My message will continue to be spread world wide. This is My Great Commission. Go out into the world. Spread My Word and My Will and MY Love to all.

I bless you. Pass this message on.

6/23/06

My dearest Ginny,

Know that I am with you and desire only the best for you when you are in My Will.

Refuse to be brought down by whatever surrounds you in this world of Mine. You are not alone. I am always with you. Continue to LISTEN to Me and to Obey. You are still often in a big rush to get moving. Cherish your time with Me and with others. Learn to see the good in yourself and in others while continuing to offer prayer for them and for yourselves.

My desire, as yours should be, is that all will be saved and spend eternity with Me in Heaven. I alone know what others need. Bring them to Me in prayer and I will do the rest. Your job is easy. I have done the work with My death on the cross. Grace abounds everywhere. People must see their need for Me and the world will be a better place and a safer one.

I alone am the answer. After people have tried the pleasures of the world and found them wanting, they may turn back to Me if people like yourself persevere in prayer and in fasting.

I love you. Go in peace

Your friend, Jesus

10/1/06

My child, I love you. Is this not enough? I put up with every sort of mistreatment to gain salvation for all. At one time you agrees to suffer for your family-you keep on forgetting about this. You ask Me for help and then you push your way through oh so many road blocks that I erect for your protection.

Pray for your family and friends. Do not be burdened by their problems or their seeming insults. Hand them directly to Me and then flow in My grace and love filled with joy and the peace which passes all understanding.

I alone am God. LISTEN to My voice. Hear and answer Me. Hear with the ears of your heart rather than your exterior ears and peace will come to you.

12/8/06

Create in me a clean heart, O Lord.

For your heart to be clean you need to desire it. I have been showing you areas of concern and you have shut Me down. Allow Me full freedom with your heart and with your soul. Behave in a manner worthy of Me. LISTEN when I speak. Continue to take issue with thoughts that intrude on our relationship. Give Me all that belongs to Me. Put Me in the first place, not the food which you put in your belly.

I love all My children, but you will not see this love until you recognize that I am your All.

Abide in Me. Let go of all other entanglements and I will show you one area at a time that needs cleansing. Until you are really ready for this clean sweep, I will allow you, as I always do, the freedom to seek you own path. Put yourself in My hands minute by minute and you will become clean and sparkling. Hold on tight. I love you.

1/6/07

Dear Lord Jesus,

I have been reading the psalms yesterday and today and feel a relationship with David when he feels overwhelmed by the abandonment of his friends. Something like Job. I see his undivided love for you as you bring an awareness of sin to him and offer him the grace of repentance. I see how often , whether in a high or a low place, he continues to offer you praise and thanksgiving. Help Me to be more aware of you when I am in the midst of a hurtful situation so that I can concentrate more and more on you and less and less on the situation.

My dearest Ginny,

Allow Me more space in your life. Pray as you did when you met ... the other day, but LISTEN when I invite you to change the subject or end the conversation. You seem to think that the goal is winning the conversation, but it is about planting seeds. If you had ended the conversation politely, you might have been able to return to it at another time. Now this is all but impossible with her.

Wait for Me to lead you in the right direction. No lead means stop and stay put. Remember I am with you always until the end of time.

2/2/07

Come, bend, LISTEN. I speak to you in the ordinary circumstances of your day. I give you opportunities to practice patience and love.

These will bring you closer to Me and to others. When you are disturbed- Pray-Pray-Pray. Let down your guard.

11/3/07

As you sit her before My Monstrance and ask for assistance, I give it to you. I love you, Ginny. I do not want you to be hurt, Move out of the way of the wall and the white washers. (EZ 13:10-15) Stay away from those who do harm by speaking against Me. Learn to spend more time alone with Me and ask Me to show you clearly whom to befriend. BE CAREFUL!

A friend is someone who likes you. He/she is someone who desires the best for and from you. A friend doesn't want the other to go through trials and burdens so will assist but not take the burden away. A friend is only human and frail and is often not available, but will step up to the plate when next available. A friend loves and then loves even more.

Friendship is very special and deserves to be nurtured with care. I alone am your best Friend. Come to Me first. I will then show you where else you may go. LISTEN CLOSELY to Me at all times.

2/2/08

Dearest Ginny,

Each time you ask Me for help I ask you to LISTEN. You do this for a while and them go off on a tangent and do your own thing. LISTENING takes concentration. Be less scattered and more focused. Share only that which you have pondered in your heart and believe deeply to be necessary. Look up at Me and away from what you perceive as problematic. Focus your love on Me and those I send on your path. Be at peace. Use this Lent to study the relationship you have with Me and My heavenly Father in the Spirit of love and peace and joy which you have never imagined.

3/21/08 Good Friday

I speak to you in this silence of My love for you. You are tryinbg to do My will, but you must stop all this trying and simply surrender your will to Mine. When I do all the work, all you need do is LISTEN and OBEY. This stops all your struggling with Me and others. Be thou My instrument of peace and recoonciliation. Forfeit your own plans and allow Me to show you My way and My will. Peace is possible for you when you let Me take the reins ans simply sit back and enjoy the ride. Sometimes it will be bumpy and other times it will be smooth, however, you will be safe because you will be covered by My blanket of love.

Go forth from here renewed in heart and spirit to do only My will in all things.

My peace is yours.

Shalom,

The Crucified Savior, Jesus, the Christ

1/30/09

Listen when I speak. Answer when I call. Do what I ask of you and you will be doing My Will and that of My Father who is in heaven. Peace-Love-Joy all abound and all are around you. Seek and find them and you will be fulfilled.

3/7/09

Is there some sort of corruption happening here and now?

My people who are called by My name have once again forsaken Me for false gods and false prophets. They are like sheep without a true shepherd following a voice they believe will take them through the turmoil. They are not discerning. They are not LISTENING for My voice in the din, and, if and when they do hear Me, they turn away and do whatever they want. When their fear becomes more of an alert for them, they may begin to LISTEN and they must have devout persons to turn to. They will need to repent and reform their lives and tighten their belts and stay close to Me and to others who really know Me. If they do not-they will perish from their own faults. They will have no one to blame, but themselves because they have become haughty and ignorant and foolish in the ways of the world. Be at peace. I am with you. LISTEN to Me more closely and follow My will at all times. Go in peace.

5/23/09

Dear Ginny,

I answer all prayer in time. LISTEN for the answer. Look closely.

6/5/09

Dear Ginny,

I love to show you My love in many and varied ways. I am pleased when you see the gifts I send you.

LISTEN to your heart and follow it. You will be led even closer to Me.

Pray unceasingly. Adore Me whenever possible. Be the best Ginny that I call you to be. Forever, I will praise the glory of God's name. Remember who you are as a child of Mine.

Comfort My little ones.

7/4/09

Guidance

Guidance is a gift

I give this gift to you

I ask you to follow it

I ask you to discern

I ask you to dedicate yourself to Me

I call on you to look on Me with love

I call you to see Me in the other

I invite you to worship Me

I show you that I am with you always

I send you out into My vineyard

I give you My grace for each task

I allow you to fail when you refuse to LISTEN

I beg that you love all who are sent your way

Live always in My grace

Love always with My Love

Forgive others as I forgive you

Chill out-be more mellow

Follow My lead and you will never be lost

Step off the path and I will guide you back if you ask

Smell the flowers and the rain along the way

Your journey is to bring you to your heavenly abode to spend eternity in My presence, comfort and care

Extend a hand and a hug to those whom you meet along the way-not just those whose hands are clean but to all those you meet

I am with you always until the end of time

Hold on—hang on when necessary

This journey is not always peaceful

Wind is necessary to drive the leaves away and to dry up the puddles

Comfort Me as you offer comfort to others—

Go in peace

9/5/09

Somewhere in the midst of all your turmoil you will find Me as I desire that you become calm and have the peace that passes all understanding. You are to enjoy it always as a way of life, but it is up to you to subject yourself to Me—to LISTEN and to OBEY, not to rebel. Find a place where you can retreat and be alone with Me and we will be able to have many quiet conversations.

9/10/09

My little child,

Continue to come to Me day and night with your trials and tribulations, your joys and your sorrows, your awareness and your questions. Allow Me to be the first one to whom you come. First LISTEN to Me and OBEY. Obedience is of prime import. Bring Me your cares and share with Me your consolations. Love Me and you will become more free and available to love others.

Share My love with everyone with whom you come in contact. At times the sole sharing, which could be soul sharing, may be as simple as a smile. You may be rejected, but please continue doing this.

Pray for those who are in darkness. Invite Me to open their eyes to the beauty which surrounds them. Shower them with loving prayer and do not annoy them. They are already in too much pain and are in need of a little relief. Prayer will help. Write their names in the book at the Monastery and leave them to Me at the foot of My cross where droplets of My blood can and will cleanse them and free them from the darkness of sin and death. Stop taking everything so personally.

5/1/10

Come to Me in the quiet

Come to Me in the dark

Come to Me when I call

Come to Me and LISTEN patiently

I will sing for you

My song is of love and peace

I care for all My children

LISTEN in the silence

I am there

I am the stone

I am the rock

I am the foundation

I am the Way and the Truth and the Life

I am the beginning and the end

I alone am God

Worship and adore Me now

5/7/10

Come to Me often and LISTEN closely and clearly. John was a man after My own heart. You are a woman on the right path much of the time. Spend more time in LISTENING before you go out and march for justice. Temporarily, I want you on the sidelines watching what is happening around you , but not acting on what you see. Do this and you will find the peace which has been alluding you. Look and LISTEN, but do not act until I give you direction. Peace.

10/6/10

I come to you in my need
You LISTEN and respond
You tell me of Your love for all
You allow Me to ramble
I come to You with a heavy heart
You lighten my load
You share it with me
You comfort and console me
I come to You filled with awe

You share even more of Yourself with me

You show me spectacular things

You cause me to be more open and aware

I come to You filled with joy

You ask me to overflow to others

You ask me to share Your peaceful

Praises abound even amid sadness

Fear is still mingled with joy

Others share and I see Yourself

There is a deep seated peace

I leave free to love and be loved

10/25/10

Rejoice

The time is near

Fear not I am with you

LISTEN to the birds

See the butterflies

Worship Me

See My face and live

Continue to grow

Storm clouds are over head

The harvest is ready

Come, visit with Me

Show others your love of Me

Smell all the fragrances

Burn rubbish and keep warm

Fly from harm

Follow My lead

I will bring you home

6/3/11

I accept you

Accept all who come to you

I send them

LISTEN to their needs

Confirm their hope

Help them with their grief

Put you on hold because I hold you
in the palm of My hand

Hold their hearts as I hold yours

Allow yourself to be vulnerable

Don't consider the cost

Don't consider who is asking

Follow My suggestions

LISTEN closely to Me

I am God

I love all

All are Mine

Cherish Me

Wear your smile and I will be seen

Forget yourself while loving others

I will soothe your pain

Use it to soothe others

Continue to love in your hurt

Bring compassion and peace

Pray for all

and

You will find the peace which has been escaping you

Live in My Love and My arms

10/22/11

Is God calling you?

Are you LISTENING to His voice?

He speaks in the depths of your heart

He has a special mission for you

He needs you to fulfill His plan

He will never leave you or forsake you

He fills you with His love

He leads you by the hand

He fills in all the gaps

He gifts you for the journey

Leave your baggage behind

Live in faith and hope

The journey will be nothing but exciting

Ask Him what He wants from you

Be willing to OBEY

You will be surprised by what

He can accomplish through you

Onward Christian soldier!

Do not let your past sins keep you down

All sin and fall short of the glory of God

Repent and then share with others

LISTEN to their trials

Share yours

Share Me

Humility is the capital virtue

It is not being a doormat

It is LISTENING to Christ and to others

It is feeling with others

It is being all of the you God called you to be

It is wisdom personified

4/11/12

If I speak with the tongues of angels

Will you LISTEN?

If I speak through a neighbor

Will you LISTEN?

If I speak in a whisper

Will you LISTEN?

You do not need a hearing aid

Your hearing needs an aid

You need to be in tune with My voice

You need to anticipate My call

You need to be aware that I speak

Open your heart

Open your mind

Open all your senses

Be open

I will speak-I do speak

5/5/12

Go into the world

Speak My words to all

LISTEN to them

Lead them to Me

Let them find Me

If I ask you to remain still

Do so

If I ask you to move out

Do so

LISTEN and OBEY

LISTEN to your heart

Discern My voice

I speak often

Keep awake and alert

5/7/12

Children LISTEN and learn

Become as a child

Learn from Me

Join with others

Pray with them

I will join you

I will pray with you

I will direct your prayer

Pray in My will

LISTEN to My voice

Reflect on My voice

Love unconditionally

You will see rewards

5/21/12

Take your time

LISTEN for My voice

I will protect you

Lean on Me

I will hold you loosely

Don't struggle

All will be well

Say nothing unkind

Be not afraid

My mother and I are with you

Relax

9/12/12

Sit beside Me and hold My hand

Clasp it firmly

Allow Me to comfort you

Allow Me to calm you

Allow Me to center you

Call My name-I LISTEN

Look at My face-I understand

Stand firm on My truth

It never changes

I will never leave you nor forsake

you

My hand is warm–let Me warm you

My hand is gentle–let Me share My gentleness

My hand is firm–let Me guide you

Let Me love you–trust in Me

10/1/12

If you hear Me, LISTEN

If you see Me, look

Look into My eyes

Hear My voice

Call My name

Do My will

Open your heart

Be vulnerable

I will not hurt you

I will soothe your pain

Be real

Be sensitive

I feel what you are feeling

I understand your guilt

I understand your fears

I LISTEN

Speak to Me

I always offer My love

Sometimes My love appears soft

Sometime I may call you on something

All of this is love

I desire your salvation

Be at peace

Confess your sins

Do your penance

Be free and soar like an eagle

Trust in Me...I am Love

10/20/12

Put on the armor of God

Be ready for battle

You have chosen My side

LISTEN to Me for direction

Follow My lead

Do not look around

The others may not be on My side

There is a hell

It is everlasting

You, alone, make your own decision

Follow Me

Keep on the straight path

When you go off path–Repent

Get up and begin again

I love you

I desire Heaven for you

Follow Me

I will give you peace

Do not worrying

10/27/12

I speak to you in the silence

You try not to LISTEN

You keep busy with prayers

Stop-Look at Me-LISTEN

I will heal you

Feel My Presence

I hear you cry

I sense your pain

Open your eyes

Look at Me

Praise Me-Glorify Me-Honor Me-
OBEY Me

Be My light in a darkened world

2/3/13

Continue LISTENING to Me

I will instruct you

I will send the opportunities

You are My servant

Do My will

Wait for the instructions

I will use you as you are

Some will LISTEN

Some will desire to change

Others will remain in place

Don't chase them down

Be where I place you

Stay on the path I carve for you

Slow down

Sometimes you miss the curves

You go off on a vector

It takes time to return to the path

This time is wasted

Slowing down is nor a waste

Slowing down is a precaution

Watch for pot holes

Go slowly around them

Don't stop to look at them

Keep your focus on Me

I am pleased with you

Be humble

Be sincere

Be Ginny

5/31/13

I have called you by name

I have given you My love

I have showered you with blessings

I have shone My Light on you

Look-LISTEN-OBEY

Carry My Light

Share it with others

LISTEN to their pain

Bring it to Me

Invite them to share it with Me

I will direct you

I will show you My plan for you

One step at a time

Ask for help when you need it

The answer will be in front of you

You will not need to travel far or wide

I will provide

I will also be your protection

Step out in faith

NOW!!

6/11/13

LISTEN to Me

I will send the Spirit

He and I are One

The Father is also One

Open yourself and receive Us

Be in the world, not of it

LISTEN to My Word

OBEY and follow

Keep your feet on the path

If you slip off-repent

I desire you to be one with Me

The way is not difficult

Keep your eyes on Me

You will be fine

Direct them elsewhere-you will fall

Keep on keeping on

I want you with Me in Heaven

My Word has strength

My Word has love

My Word heals

My Word has power

My Word soothes

My Word has all the answers

Open your Book

Read-LISTEN-Learn

Receive grace and peace

10/20/13

When you attend

I LISTEN

When you commit

I help you

When you love Me

I love you tenderly

When you choose Me

You choose Eternal Life

10/26/13

I have risen from the dead

I am alive!

You also are alive in Me

Live in Me

Act with My Love

Keep My commandments

Do My Will

LISTEN to My voice

Fall more in love with Me

Spend more time in My Presence

Affirm one another

Walk in My Word

Keep the peace

Go in peace

11/1/13

Many are called; few are chosen

Be My disciples

LISTEN to My Word

Carry it to others

Do My Will

I will assist you

Be open to My call

I call at all hours–day and night

I ask you to do My Will

I give you the ability

Don't say you are incapable

I will supply all the tools you need

Fear not; I am with you

Love others as I love you

Be open and receptive

Keep My commandments

Show others My Way

It may not be easy

It may be extremely difficult

Persevere

Eternity with Me is the desired end

Seeing Me face to face is worth the trials

Endure

11/15/13

Come to Me all you who labor

Peace is yours

Love is yours

Be humble

Put Me first

LISTEN when I call

Prompt others

Feel My pain

Do My Will

All I have is yours

Just ask

1/7/14

When you sit and look at Me

I LISTEN

When you call on Me

I hear

I am never away from you

I am always available

Don't hesitate

Don't worry about bothering Me

I look-I LISTEN-I love

Look-LISTEN-love

Respond to My calls

I always respond to yours

Be with Me

Seek Me more often

Meditate

3/1/14

LISTEN to the silence

Silence the noise

3/18/14

Abide in Me

Rest in My arms

Throw away pre-conceived notions

Be always open to My Will

LISTEN carefully

Stop rushing around

Stay put

Love Me

Allow Me to love you

Drink of My virtues

Be at peace

Be serene

I will surprise you

You need not be on guard

You need to be relaxed

Open your heart

I will fill it

4/3/14

If you listen; I will speak

Lean not on your own understanding

Trust in Me

I will give you peace

Share your burdens

Carry the pain of others

Let them carry yours

Be fruitful

Multiply your prayers

Search for Me

I am beside you

Feel My Presence

Ask what you will

Be in tune with My Will

Cast your burden on Me

I will give you strength

I will soothe your pain

I will fill your loneliness

I will strengthen your faith

I alone know the outcome

All will be My Will

Be still and know

I offer you My strength

Be prepared for the journey

I am with all of you

You will be refreshed

You will not understand

4/4/14

You are welcome

To come into My house

To pray-to sing-to meditate

Leave Me your fears and your dreams

Return home with your burdens lifted

Share your plans and your hopes with Me

I LISTEN and I respond

Leave your worries behind

Free from your burdens

You will be free to minister to others

Lead them to Me

They are also welcome

Leave in and at peace

4/8/14

I called to you

You responded

I choose to speak to you now

LISTEN carefully

I am here with you

I surround you with Love

I choose to Love you

Become more vulnerable again

Let others get under your skin

LISTEN to their pain

Expect to be rejected

I was

Never underestimate My Power

I see you. I know you

Be kind, and gentle and open

Be vulnerable; I was

Love, love, love

Give without expecting

I have and will continue to protect you

See the good in others

Speak to them about Me

Show them the path to righteousness

Fear not, I am with you

4/19/14

I Am the Bread of Life

I Am here for you

Eat of Me and live

I am the Vine

Cling to Me and

You shall have everlasting life

Call to Me

LISTEN when I answer

Bring Me to others!

Show them My Love

Go and gather more disciples

Follow Me

I lead the way

Be at peace

The darkness will not overcome My Light

5/3/14

Repent-Reform-Receive

Open your heart wide

Allow Me to come inside

I love you I cherish you

Come also into My heart

LISTEN to the beat of My heart

Stay in sync with Me

In this way you will be

Safe-Warm-Protected-Saved

Don't become childish

Do become child like

Come right up to Me

Ask anything you want

I will always LISTEN

I will give you what is best

Be thankful and at peace

I call you to holiness

This is the reason I was crucified

LISTEN to My cry

LISTEN for My call

Do My Will

Eternity has been earned for you

5/23/14

Follow Me

I will lead you

LISTEN to your heart

I speak to you there

Your day will be filled

I am in it

I am in you

I am in the other

Silence the voices from your past

Live in the moment

Look forward

Love and be loved

5/25/14

If you live with Me

and

If you love Me

I will stay with you

Do not stray

Stay on the path I lay before you

LISTEN to My voice

Heed My call

Do My will

Stop perseverating

Move forward

Keep the past in perspective

Learn from it

Move forward

I was in the past

I am in the present

I will be in the future

Keep your eyes focused on Me

Turn your ears to My voice

Keep your feet on My path

This path will twist and turn

I will lead you

Do not fear

I am with you

Even if you should fall

I am with you

Stop-Look-LISTEN

I am your All in All

Relax

Go with My flow

Amen-Alleluia

Bienvenue

5/27/14

I will save you

I will protect you

LISTEN to My Word

Heed My voice

Follow My Way

Do not stray

Do not struggle

Go Forward in love and peace

I am with you

I will never leave you

or

Forsake you

Be My apostle

Share My Word and My Truth

Onward Christian Soldier

8/2/14

I give you direction

I show you My Way

Listen carefully

I may speak quietly

9/5/14

You have LISTENED to My Voice

You have heard My Word

You have OBEYED Me

You offered your suffering

I accepted your offering

Continue to offer

I will sustain you

I will send My grace to you

It will not be easy

It may not even be pleasant

I know what I asked of you

I will sustain you

Hold on tightly

The ride may be uneven

I will sustain you

Pray for them

Pray even more

I hear your prayer

I direct it to others

The outcome is not yours

It is not for you to know

Go when and where I direct you

I will sustain you

You are not going this alone

Others have and will join you

They have offered to pray

I alone know the outcome

I do not force the will of anyone

I will sustain you

Recall only the good

Leave the bad behind

Keep on letting go

I will sustain you

Pray-Pray-Pray

Relax-Rest-Abide

I will conquer

Leave it all to Me

I will sustain you

9/7/14

Why do you doubt?

Do you not trust Me?

You say that you do

You still keep yourself wound up

You are not resting in Me

I speak to you

You do LISTEN

You do not put My words into action

You still desire to be in control

I will allow this

Try to apply what I say

Give yourself permission to be free

Free yourself from you

Focus only on Me

Allow Me to absorb the darts

I have already died for you

It is your turn to die to Me

11/1/14

Beware of false prophets

Beware of false priests

Beware of false believers

They are among you

Know My Truth

Know My Love

Do not be deceived

They are very clever

Some deceive even themselves

Stay close to Me

Stay close to My mother, Mary

Stay close to My Church

Keep your soul and body pure

Share your purity with others

Come, Follow, Relax

Agitation will not help you

Be at peace

Stay close; then, come even closer

Stay the course

Invite others to join you

Disaster may come

Death is not your enemy

Heaven is your goal

Stay the course

Do not be discouraged

Continue smiling and singing

Continue praying and admonishing

You will not be guilty if you speak
the truth

I will hold you accountable

Only if you refuse to uphold Me

Keep on keeping on

Keep yourself in shape spiritually and physically

I need soldiers who are fit to serve

LISTEN even more closely

This will require more quiet time

Spend more time alone with Me

Read–Meditate–Think of me

I will inspire you

Go and do My Will

Hasten slowly

11/2/14

When you are obedient

I speak to you

I send you My Love

I give you My Grace

I shower you with My Blessings

Stay the course

Do not deviate

LISTEN closely for My Will

You will head in the right direction

When you go off course; I redirect you

When you go off course; you sin

When you are out of My Will, this is sin

The closer you come to Me

The more accountable you are to Me

11/27/14

You are full now

You ate a delicious meal

You met others

You shared

You visited

You drove someone home

You were emptied

I filled you

You spilled over to others

Continue in this way

It is similar to breathing in and out

It will become second nature

LISTEN-I will direct you

12/5/14

I speak with the Tongues of men and angels

I speak of peace

I speak of love

I speak of repentance

I speak through others

I speak through friends

I speak through enemies

Are you LISTENING?

2/20/15

Look inside

I have given you the answer

Call on Me

Be less impetuous

Confirm My call

Relax

Take good care of yourself

Be at peace

I will care for the others

Everyone is not in your care

LISTEN to your heart

Use fewer words

Be at peace

3/1/15

Set My people free

Show them My Way

Be MY torch bearer

Shine My Light

Pray-Pray-Pray

Invite others to join you

In obedience to Me

LISTEN ever more closely

I will speak to you

I do speak to you

Proceed in my grace

3/28/15

Invite Me

I will eat at your table

I will dine with you

I will converse with you

I will answer your questions

I will LISTEN to your problems

I will show you My Way

Be at peace

Eat leisurely

Sup some wine

Be relaxed

Get to really know Me

Get to really know yourself

Get ready to meet Me personally

Set the table

Light some candles

Take your time

Escape from distractions

Let us be alone together

Turn off the television

Shut the book

Abide with Me

4/4/15

I speak to your heart

LISTEN intently

I speak to your soul

Be open to Me

I give you My peace

Receive it freely

5/5/15

I catch your tears

I hear you cry

I LISTEN to your requests

Keep on your path to Me

LISTEN to the truth

Continue to pray for the wayward

I give them My grace

I show them My Way

They have free will

They go their own way

I continue to send them grace

One day they may find My path again

5/17/15

Stay close to Me

Do not stray

Keep My Words in your mind

Recite My Words with your mouth

Listen to My mother

She intercedes with Me

Show her your love

Show her your commitment

Renew your consecration

We are here for you

Don't hesitate to ask

Remember to praise and thank

Every day is a new beginning

Begin again

7/14/15

When I speak many LISTEN

Not many follow or OBEY

Listen with your heart

Listen with your mind

Ask Me to elaborate

Check with the teachings of the Church

Become well informed

Do not grasp at straws

Inform your conscience

Seek spiritual guidance

Try not to be clever

Be certain

Persevere in My Truth

Stay on My Path

Buddy up with MY people

Pray and then pray more

Seek Me out

LISTEN-OBEY-TRUST-PERSEVERE

7/28/15

Bear My burdens

Help Me carry the load

Pray for those who offend Me

Pray for those who hurt you

Take action only when I say

I will nudge you to go forward

I will hold you when you are to stay

LISTEN even more closely

Do absolutely nothing alone

Always check in with Me

I will be clear

If you have no clarity-stay put

Keep on asking for My assistance

Keep on LISTENING for answers

Be quiet and wait

This will bring you peace

Trust Me

8/1/15

Are you LISTENING?

Do you hear MY Voice?

Do you OBEY?

Do you follow My Way?

8/8/15

LISTEN the first time I call

Don't make Me call again

Don't shut Me out

Don't hang up on Me

Do discerning

Do check that it is I who has called

Use your spiritual caller ID

Does it fit with My guidelines?

Is it possible?

Is it doable?

Then proceed in faith

The outcome is not in your hands

You are in My hands

I will protect you from yourself

I will guide and direct you

Just do it when I call

When you are obedient;

Expect more calls more often

I will use you for My Work

9/5/15

Take My hand

Walk with Me

Talk with Me

Slow down

No need to run

I am always available

I LISTEN

I respond

I bring you peace

Enjoy My beauty

Enjoy yourself

Follow Me

I will lead you home

I will support you

Lean on Me

I am your stability

Feel My Presence

Be at peaceful

9/22/15

I called you here

You LISTENED

Go on your way in peace

I have heard your prayers

I will give My grace

Others must be willing to receive

Keep on praying

Do not give up

Persevere

Do you trust Me?

Let it go

Continue on your journey

9/27/15

Take it easy

Proceed with caution

LISTEN for My direction

Stop if I tell you

Be aware

Seek d/irection

10/3/15

I work quietly....unseen

I speak to the depths of your heart

I expect you to LISTEN

I expect you to act

Do not delay

Be open and available

Go to your interior

Stay there longer

Wait for Me to speak

I speak words of wisdom and truth

I speak of My Love and Mercy

I speak of forgiveness and Truth

LISTEN more closely

I do give you direction

Be not afraid

I will accompany you

I do desire gentleness

Let Me do a big work in you

Let others see the difference

Go in peace

I am with you always

Until the end of time

10/24/15

I feel your pain

I hear your call

I LISTEN

I allow you to be in pain

LISTEN more closely in your pain

You will hear more deeply

You will have deeper clarification

You will have more compassion

You will sense My Love

You will be shown a better you

I love you

Relax, rest, sense My Love

Go in peace, slowly

11/7/15

I hear your call

I hear you sigh

I see the look on your face

I feel your muscles tighten

I LISTEN

I respond

Your pain is transformed to joy

Your muscles relax

You are free

12/25/15

I come to you in the silence

I offer you My Grace

Accept it

Give it to others

It will then continue to grow in you

Fill yourself with My Love

Give it away

You will become even fuller

Do not hesitate

Do My Will

LISTEN closely to My whispers

Live in the moment

Be Mine always

1/6/16

Thank you for your obedience

Search diligently for the truth

Share it with others

Let them process it themselves

Move to where I sent you

Continue to reach out to others

You will never know the results

Many will appear to ignore you

Some will LISTEN intently

All will be changed by the encounter

This includes you

Go in peace-relax-share

THE END for now

Any comments or compliments
please contact me

Ginny-K-Allen@hotmail.com

Check out my other books

Broken and Bruised...Holy and
Sanctified

Cme-Follow-Relax

May God Bless you